Lisa's case for a heart revival provokes thought, inspires change, and spreads a hopeful message: God is not hiding; he wants to be found by those who want him. Lisa vulnerably guides the reader toward this truth, which fosters a deeper love of God, a more intimate knowledge of who he is, and an understanding of why we want him.

Mark Batterson,
New York Times bestselling author of *The Circle Maker*

This book resonates with the deepest cry of my heart.

Sheila Walsh,
Bible teacher and bestselling author

I turned the first page, devoured the rest, and here I am...speechless. The reading of *I Want God* is a wrecking and a revival and a resurrection, all at once.

Jill Kelly,
New York Times bestselling author and speaker

Reconstructive heart surgery. *I Want God* not only provides new life for your weary, worn-out soul, but it motivates you to exchange a lesser life for one that hungers after true joy. Written by a flawed and honest pilgrim, Lisa Whittle has walked this path toward soul revival before, and like a kindly guide, ushers us toward the renewed life in Jesus we've always longed for.

Mary DeMuth,
author of *The Wall Around Your Heart*

Lisa Whittle's writing strikes to the center of who we are meant to be. I am inspired and moved and deeply grateful for how she pours her heart out on every page. This book is no exception.

Annie F. Downs,
author of *Let's All Be Brave*

This is not an easy read, and that is the highest compliment I can pay Lisa in her carefully penned but drastically bold work *I Want God*. If you feel like you have everything and at the same time you have nothing, read this book. It is a proclamation, a manifesto, and a rally-cry for those of us who are weary and hungry. Be warned: saying "I Want God" will require much of you. In return, God will bring a revival to your heart and an abundance of Himself to the empty spaces around you. He will bring healing and hope.

Anne Marie Miller,
Bible teacher and author of
Permission to Speak Freely and *Lean on Me*

Lisa Whittle

G**I Want**D

HARVEST HOUSE PUBLISHERS
EUGENE, OREGON

Cover by Harvest House Publishers, Inc., Eugene, Oregon

Published in association with the literary agency of The FEDD Agency, Inc., PO Box 341973, Austin, TX 78734.

I WANT GOD
Copyright © 2014 by Lisa Whittle
Published by Harvest House Publishers
Eugene, Oregon 97402
www.harvesthousepublishers.com

Library of Congress Cataloging-in-Publication Data
Whittle, Lisa.
I want God / Lisa Whittle.
    pages cm
ISBN 978-0-7369-5920-9 (pbk.)
ISBN 978-0-7369-5921-6 (eBook)
1. Christian women—Religious life. 2. Spirituality—Christianity. 3. God (Christianity)
I. Title.
BV4527.W4984 2014
248.8'43—dc23

2014002435

Printed in the United States of America

14 15 16 17 18 19 20 21 22 / VP-JH / 10 9 8 7 6 5 4 3 2 1

> "I can no other answer make but thanks,
> and thanks; and ever thanks."
> *Shakespeare*

Scotty, Graham, Micah, and Shae, my four favorite people on the planet: *You were the family I dreamed of when I was a little girl. Let's keep having fun, together.*

Family and Friends: *I love you. Thank you for praying and cheering.*

LaRae: *For so many years I've liked you. Now we get to partner. Pure joy.*

Kathleen: *You were God-sent. Thank you for words of affirmation and honest critique. I adore you, woman.*

Esther: *This was the right book with the right people at the right time. Thanks for tirelessly pursuing it with me.*

Women at New Vision Church in Murfreesboro, Tennessee: *I stood before you and promised if this became a book I would put you in it. Thanks for being willing to hear the message first. I think of your faces and stories, often.*

Reader: *Whether you bought this book or someone gave it to you, it's now in your hands. Thank you for investing your time in its pages. May God speak loud and clear.*

And yesterday, today, and forevermore, thanks be to my Jesus. *As long as I can remember, it's always been us. Thank You.*

To Momma

Who has always wanted God most

Contents

Introduction

I spend the first three months after my last book, *{w}hole*, releases picking emotional shrapnel out of my skin. It is a hard book to write; I honestly do not know if I ever want to write again.

When something is hard it is an instinct to get lost in the tall-tree forest of the daily—to hide behind carpool lines, grocery store visits, texts, smartphone games, and washing dirty laundry. We settle into predictability, like standing trunks that don't change. The days we live look exactly like they did many days before.

But then I remember what living in the tall trees before has helped me learn: The only way I know to get better is to focus on God harder.

So I come out of hiding and write this book.

———•———

Since you are reading *I Want God*, I imagine one of four things to be true of you. Either you are in a place of *lack*—the starving, desperate, need-God-to-consume-you-more-than-what-is-currently-consuming-your-life place; you are in a place of plenty but it is not satisfying and you still want more; you are spiritually dead and have no clue how to change it; or you are on a search for what you think may be the missing piece of your life. It doesn't matter which. Your soul is in need of revival.

Join the crowd.

There are a lot of us, Christians, out there today. We are short and tall and blonde and dark-skinned and happy and sad and good and sometimes mean as a snake. We park our cars in parking spaces, buy milk at the store and convenience store Cokes, plant flowers in our yard and lay some of them on loved ones' gravestones. We work at jobs, stand in unemployment lines and sit in dentists' waiting rooms, ride roller coasters with arms in the air and on different days, worship God in big church rooms and small family rooms with arms lifted there, too. We are living, yes. But many of us aren't living very well when it comes to our relationship with God.

For some of us He's there but not really, makes the short list but not #1. We visit Him on Sundays, preach Him on Twitter, bake cookies to take to neighbors "in His name"…but never find the right moment to talk to them about Who and what and why. For others of us, life is good and we are busy. Or life is hard and we are wounded by the saviors we trusted to do the job, but didn't.

At some point, we ran into the forest of the daily and got lost. We have hidden in the tall trees long enough. We need to come out so we can get better.

But this book is not a book about need.

This is a book about *want*.

There is a reason it is called *I Want God*.

Because, you see, you and I both know in that deep-down place…we are selfish. And even things we know we *need* we do not always get because we do not really *want* them.

We *need* to be healthier, but we do not *want* to exercise.

We *need* to be wiser with our money, but we do not *want* to stop spending.

We *need* to have better communication with our family, but we do not *want* to take the time to sit down and talk.

We *need* more of God, but we do not really *want* Him.

The truth is, until the want matches the need, nothing will ever change. Needing without wanting is just a really good idea that never sees light.

We can talk about social justice issues, promote spiritual causes and service, but until we want God the very most our ministries will merely be good efforts. I have known many people who didn't want God but racked up countless mission hours doing things that were very good. I've also known people who love God but never do much to serve Him. Yet I have never known a true, passionate God-wanter whose relationship did not overflow into great Kingdom usefulness. Just try to get a Jesus freak to sit on their hands and do nothing. It will never work.

> When we want Him and experience a soul revival, there is no limit to what we will do for Him.

That is why wanting God is so important: When we want Him and experience a soul revival, there is no limit to what we will do for Him. We will find ourselves in the world of *I never thought I'd do this but I couldn't do anything else even if I tried.* When we taste of the good thing it will ruin our palates; we will never again be satisfied with the mediocre. We will come out from hiding behind the predictability of tree trunks and realize that as safe as the tall-tree forest at one time seemed, its staleness makes us go mad. Wanting God is not a risk. Living without wanting Him is.

But do not think for one minute that we aren't going to walk this out together. The world doesn't need any more experts, and an expert does not write this book. The world needs passionate and focused people who are willing to be honest about their own struggle and share what they learn on their quest to be better. It is from this place that I write this book. In community, we will seek out this revival.

Yet it will start in *each* of our souls.

And what does that really mean—that in our soul we have revival?

It means that because of Jesus, we are not too far gone. There are things we want more than God that keep us from wanting Him most. Those things consume us. We need to identify them, pray, and get rid of them. Those life-changing steps aren't easy, but they're not impossible. They will restore us to God and He will do a miraculous work within.

And at the end of it all? It is my prayer that we will not only be filled with joy and hope and purpose in a way we have never before realized, but we will be consumed with an endless and ravenous passion for God, able to say, as did King David while living in a dark, dungy cave, "I pray to you, O Lord. I say, 'You are my place of refuge. **You are all I really want in life**'" (Psalm 142:5).

Oh God…*may it be so.*

Lisa Whittle
January 2014

Something You
Should Know First

On the day in early 2012 when my pursuit of wanting God begins, I write a blog post (included in the back of this book). Despite the messy housewife staring back at me in the mirror, I feel like an old-time preacher about to walk into a puffy white tent and preach my guts out in a revival. I cannot explain this, other than to say it is the unsolicited visual God gives me as I begin to write.

Since images like this do not come to me in my everyday laundry washing, carpool driving, dinner cooking life, I know I have to pay attention.

I begin to study revivals, and particularly the Welsh Revival of 1904-1905. I'm intrigued by it partly because the movement's beginning is credited to a young woman, Florrie Evans, and partly because it is a piece of history I do not know. I read for what seems like hours, my mouth wide the whole time over what I learn. Over 100,000 people saved. Bars and brothels shut down, people worshipping God for hours and days, sports stadiums empty because the players and fans are present, instead, in church. I am an everyday woman, but I want that radical movement of God again. I want that movement of God inside of me.

As I read about the Welsh Revival, my questions are these: How does God create such movement? What makes for such extraordinary movements of God? Can it happen again? In the ordinary people I read about, I find answers: the everyday invitation for God to come in and bring the radical, the surrender, the willingness to want Him most in life—things we can all do.

I'll share more about the Welsh Revival in every chapter of this book. May their experience be our teacher.

I Want God
More

What do you want?
JOHN 1:38

I sit, wringing sweaty six-year-old hands in the backseat of Momma's massive '70s boat on wheels, trying to muster the courage to tell her I've met God.

She is the least judgmental person I know and the one who loves Him most. But I remember our recent talk in the yellow kitchen about not asking Him into my heart because it is the good girl thing to do but waiting until I really want Him, and I fear she may think I'm not ready.

We are in the parking lot of Judon's Hotdogs and we have just been to night church. My mind is still dancing over what has taken place that evening inside the stained glass walls—the glorious but curious display of Jesus. Church people I know in ninja-looking head sashes; hairy men's feet stuffed in Walmart sandals meant to look Roman. Grown adults and young children with pumped fists shaking, saying words they don't mean, like "Crucify Him," portraying the *back then* crowd.

Someone calls this curious display of

> **Bottom Line**
>
> Forget other things. But never, ever forget God.

13

Jesus a passion play, and I overhear it. I am intrigued; it is the first passion play I have ever seen.

By the time the play ends and my daddy's best preacher voice booms through the worship room to invite those who don't know Christ to accept Him, my heart is a whirlpool, and I am twirling inside.

It is the impatient sound of my brother's voice claiming starvation that cuts through these thoughts. I stop spinning long enough to travel back to the backseat.

"I am *so* hungry," he laments in my ear. I bob to the surface to inhale real life in the scent of a foot-long hotdog. I don't want it, and that surprises me. Judon's hotdogs are among my favorite things in the world.

But I'm too busy thinking about Walmart sandals meant to look Roman, the eyes of a guy playing Jesus, and my best friend, Kathy.

Kathy is playful and funny, and I feel playful and funny when I am with her. Her daddy is a deacon, which makes us a perfect pair. Thinking about her sweeps me away to the things that just took place, and suddenly, I have rewound so far that the night's events are starting over.

We enter the worship room and take our seats in the front row, eager for the Jesus show. The lights dim and the show begins and I think Kathy is watching, but I'm not sure. I hope she is, because I'll need to talk to her later about what my eyes are recording. I'm glued to the display of scenes Daddy and Momma have read to me out of that enormous white family Bible—scenes that didn't wear reality until now…and I am all in, start to finish.

It is after the Jesus-man has ascended in a white robe, upward, in a billowing cloud of smoke to loud claps and cheers that my daddy speaks in his preacher voice and I hear Kathy. Daddy has taken the stage to tell people they too can know this Jesus, and to repeat his words with their lips and heart. With his every word, Kathy is repeating them—soft enough for only me to hear, but to me they sound megaphoned.

Dear Jesus…I know I am a sinner…please come into my life and save me…

It's a weird voice she's using, and I don't like it. It sounds silly and sing-y and not at all like it's coming from her. A giggle escapes and I know for sure it is something she is saying to be funny and not something that is real.

My six-year-old heart, which knows nothing of the Pharisee, feels grieved and righteous. How can Kathy pretend to mean such important words when God can hear them? I am embarrassed for both of us and worried my father will hear her and give us *the look*—the one I've seen him give teenagers in the church sometimes when they are being loud.

But more than anything, I'm wondering why I feel something so strong it is squeezing the breath from me, something of crosses and angry crowds and Jesus and small, young me. I have heard about this Savior many times already, but I've never really *seen* Him…and I am aware for the first time that my universe is about more than playing with stray kittens in my tree house fort outside my country home.

I want God. For the first time. And it consumes every six-year-old square inch of me.

I want to know Him and touch Him and never hurt His heart.

I want to love Him and feel His love back.

I want to talk to Him, like they say I can, with the simple words I know.

I want to be funny about other things, but never about Him on a cross.

I want to tell God I want Him and **I want to mean it.**

And so, with loud voice in heart, I repeat the words my preacher daddy is saying where only God can hear them. I have shuttered my eyelids closed so I won't see Kathy or anyone else; I want no distractions. I am more serious about Jesus than my years say I should be, more serious than I've ever been about anything else. I feel like a sprinter running toward something grand, and it makes me feel brave and full and honest.

I want God, and I want Him to know it.

With little girl courage and tiny, sweaty palms, I repeat these things and the whole story to my momma from the backseat of her boat on wheels in the parking lot of Judon's Hotdogs.

And while the hotdogs get cold and my voice tells the way I met Jesus, my momma cries like all mommas who want their kids to know the Great One do.

Forgetting

For me, as for you, it is important to remember our first encounter with Jesus. Because as calendar days fly away and life becomes noisy, those of us who know God often forget how bad we once wanted Him.

Maybe then the irony is true: that we who have much are often the most in need because we have forgotten how it feels to be desperate.

And let's be honest. It almost seems unfair of God to stick us in a world where we are likely to fail to live the 1 Corinthians 7:31 life—the *those who use the things of this world should not become attached to them* life. That's a near impossibility and seems to just get harder with every new gadget, every activity, every house built in the suburbs, every child born into a world that tells them they are entitled. We struggle with having so much we want and at the same time, still wanting God.

> We who have much are often the most in need because we have forgotten how it feels to be desperate.

So it is of no surprise that we *are* surprised when we remember Him and the want stirs. We walk by the mirror one day and catch a glimpse of fixed hair and lipsticked lips and ties with perfect knots nestled in crisp, collared shirts, and what we see looks crude and incomplete. And we wonder why we have never noticed before how perfection can be so flawed and how comfort can feel so uncomfortable, and we mourn the life we have right in front of us. And something inside us longs to take the back of our hand and smear off the lipstick, pull off the tie, rattle the everyday stale life cage we've found ourselves in, run into the street, find the pulse again—the pulse that has us beating to the wild of God.

But instead life ticks, and numbly, we move to it. The stirring gets pushed into an emotional trash compactor that keeps packing it down, deeper, to make room for more stuff—schedules, carpools, calculated risk. Before we leave the image in the mirror we make quick promises about how one day we will change and become *all in for You, God*, only we don't use those words because those words require us to take action. We say instead, *tomorrow I'll be better*, with the reservation of a half-heart that is torn between the now life and the one that started when we first drank Truth.

We walk away, and we forget.

We forget what it feels like to come with open hands and heart. How we were once awed by the Story of *in the beginning, water into wine, love held by nails, the veil torn, resurrected life*. We forget the power and the commitment, the beauty and the magnitude, the promises, the relationship, the raw passion for the cause and the reason and the immaculate, saving grace.

We forget God.

And sometimes, when the missionary comes to church with pictures, when the neighbor adopts and we touch the baby skin of a child born of a different mother, we catch that small glimpse of Him, again, and remember how we've forgotten. And our throats swell and the limbs tingle as they begin to regain their feeling, stirred by the greatness we recall. And more than anything else we want to *want*, but the want seems unfamiliar and scary and speaks harshly to the spiritual rigor mortis that has set in from years of forgetting. So instead, we just *do*.

We write out a *be better plan*.

We read a *be better book*.

We follow someone's *be better strategy*.

We pursue *being better* in ways we know and can control.

But what we don't remember is that the people who go hard for God are not the ones who try the hardest. They are the ones who want Him more than anything else.

More

We learn a lot by asking the right questions.

My friend Monty does this—asks good questions, learns a lot. It is in a car that I first encounter his game of inquisition, on a windy road between trees and more trees, tires humming me to sleep. He suggests a game of questions and I dive blindly in, grateful for the break in monotony.

The questions come in a variety pack, from *If you could have any other first name, what would it be?* to *If you could do anything and it weren't a sin, what would you do?* My husband, driving, answers them too, much to my intrigue. *He would want his name to be Austin?* Interesting, what even ten years of marriage do not let you know.

I am learning things about me too, how little I know of the things I don't need to consider in my daily life. *Where would I want to be stranded if my plane crashed and I survived?* (Silly, the pragmatist says in me, because I wouldn't.) *What would I want to eat if I could only eat one thing for the rest of my life?* (Not one thing in those terms sounds good enough, by the way.) Monty is asking the right questions—the ones that have me interested and stirred and most of all, *thinking*.

It reminds me of something similar from my sessions on the white couch of a shrink in my twenties. My father, who pastored a

megachurch, had just lost his position over a scandal that sent me reeling and left me needing to talk. Even with all his degreed smarts, the
counselor I thought a genius needed only to ask me the right questions to lead me down a path to my own self-discovery. It was all in
the *good questions* he asked.

And God—He thought the whole thing up. It was His idea to
teach loud lessons wrapped in subtle questions, for He knew that if
He asked them, we would be convicted, stirred, dialed into our own
truth. He did this a lot—asked questions to illustrate truth. One such
example that I love, chronicled in the book of John:

A wild, redolent guy who eats bugs and dresses ridiculously is out
and about, telling people that "The one who is the true light, who gives
light to everyone, was coming into the world" (John 1:9). They call
him John the Baptist, which makes me smile, wondering what kind
of church, Baptist or otherwise, would actually open its doors to let
him in. There is no other way to put it: The guy is weird. But he is the
perfect non-stereotypical messenger of Jesus, for God rarely uses the
one we'd expect.

I picture him with curly brown kudzu knuckles on wide fingers
and mad-looking moles on his skin. My mind draws him as a homeless version of Gaston, the burly bad guy in that Disney movie, sans
the singing. But of this I'm sure: He is a bass, and a loud one.

> As Jesus walked by, John looked at him and declared,
> "Look! There is the Lamb of God!" (John 1:36).

John spoke, with full lungs and heart, pointing to the Way. And
those within earshot, even his own followers, responded.

> When John's two disciples heard this, they followed Jesus
> (John 1:37).

I am moved by things in this story in this order: the breathless introduction of John's awaited Savior; the disciples' immediate decision to follow Him; and the obedience of John to faithfully preach Truth and yet, without hesitation, turn over the spotlight to the One who was greater.

The immediate reaction and obedience part moves me because I, myself, ask God to prove Himself a lot. And don't we all? Don't we ask Him to *show us, please, just one more time, You are real and You hear us and know of our need and can and will be enough,* especially in the hard times that require hardcore faith? We are the walkers on the Road to Emmaus who have seen the nail-pierced hands and feet and "still...[stand] there in disbelief" (Luke 24:41). Aren't we quick to jump toward Jesus but slow to walk the journey out with Him? The longer I have lived the more I have seen how we are more alike than we think, so I suspect I am not the only one.

He knows this about us, and much more. He knows it is in the heart of people to step quickly without understanding what stepping out really means. He wants us to dive inside to the deepest part where we know why we will follow Him and how we are willing to commit our lives to match our easy words. And He knows that it is in the right question that a soul twists and grapples and, in one way or another, responds to the lesson tucked inside.

And so, like Monty on the road trip and the shrink with the white couch, He asks His new followers the right question.

> Jesus looked around and saw them following. "What do you want?" he asked them (John 1:38).

On a spiritual day, I know the answer: "You, Lord! I want You!" is to be the cry pushed off the tongue of one of His, even a newbie. But the men in the Bible story do not answer, maybe because they do not really know.

I pause now, chewing on this: An omniscient being would not ask a question He could not answer, for there is nothing He does not know. If He asks a question, it's only to open a narrower mind to a bigger view—His—that He will reveal in the right time.

> He knows it is in the heart of people to step quickly without understanding what stepping out really means.

And now the question turns to you. *What do you want?* It's a question loaded with rich truth about who He is and what following Him is not and knowing the difference. It's a question to make us think and not just respond with a kneejerk, as we are so quick to do. It is not the want stirred by causes we hear of and needs we see and church people back from a mission trip who have slides to prove that real people are starving that suddenly turns us into rescuers and missionaries. It is the permanent kind, the unwavering kind of want…the kind of want that changes our life and helps us change others.

When He asks, "What do you want?" Jesus is asking us, *What do you really want for your life, because you have to know this going in. You can't just follow Me without understanding what following Me means, and at some point you have to stop being constantly stirred but never compelled enough to take action.*

Do you want the now life? Or do you want Me more than anything else? Having Me will be the greatest fulfillment of your life, but fulfilling doesn't always mean pain-free. Do you want to be the normal, everyday person who is flawed and doesn't have life all together but watches God do amazing things through your life?

Be warned: If you want Me most, your life might be shipwrecked. But in the midst of the storm, you'll feel My breath on your skin. You'll drink from a bitter cup of physical loss, but you'll also drink in My blood. Do you want the privilege of walking beside Me, skin to skin close, but walking away from position and comfort and wealth and all the things that are supposed to make you happy? Are you ready for the Jesus life? There's joy here, but not always happiness—not in the temporary sense, at least.

God help us, this is tough, but we cannot continue to be stirred for the moment lest we continue to dip only our toe in the pool of faith, teasing God, not being serious about wanting Him.

Earthly people that we are, we have it wrong. Because "more" is not about excess or greater possession, despite all the messages we are sent. Those who have more in the physical sense can testify to the futility of it all—how we can have so much yet none of it is enough. King Solomon talks about this in Ecclesiastes 2—how the world's "more" looks good on the outside but winds up being an empty wrapper. The "more" God gives is really about loss and less and the willingness to do without and yes, the *joy* in that. It's about discipline and dedication and focus and surrender. That's messy and that's gritty and we don't always like it, but it's the Gospel Truth.

And what makes all this hard stuff worth it? Only, always Him. God knows, we won't always be living the soothing words of the Psalms. We'll be living the agonized words of Nehemiah, Jeremiah, and Lamentations that are miraculously still able to say with a loud voice, "I want God."

And praise be to Him that just about the time we feel helpless, drowning, incapable of making such a proclamation of wanting Him, He blows in with a hopeful, resuscitating wind and—mouth on mouth—*revives us.* This is the glory of traveling with the Life— how He breathes vitality in dead spaces and offers His marvelous, illuminating light in places that are dark. And when we're in those dark places, we want God in big heaps and not small portions, because pain doesn't ever truly get better without Him. The more we have of Him, the more we survive and even thrive; the more beauty we extract from life. As my friend Pastor Teri Furr said recently, "The abundance of our life here on earth is about how much we interact with the Keeper of Eternity." Yes, Pastor Teri. Yes.

Rest assured, God does not choose to withhold Himself from us in a cat and mouse game. When the Father does not show Himself the way we ask, it is not because it is in His heart not to; it is because only He knows the time when our hearts are truly ready to *see*.

To have Him, we must want Him—more than the friends, the family, the wealth, the applause, the acceptance, the comfort. There can be nothing—even our own life—that we want more. We can't want our life and want God at the same time.

To have Him as He promises—in the full (John 10:10)—we must want Him in the same way. Full on, all the way, with all our heart. This doesn't mean sounding spiritual or quoting from the Bible. It means the surrender of everything, even the secret things we keep close and hidden. Since He is the keeper of our hearts, He knows when it is truly all His. He's heard us make halfway commitments before. He's heard us say "I need to" until we're blue in the face. And He knows that when trouble comes, our intentions will not be enough to keep us upright. It will take a fully committed heart to keep us grounded and on the path.

We cannot want God with conditions. When we say words like *anything for You, God,* but we mean *anything but this, God,* His heart is grieved. He denies this conditional allegiance of holding on to both when He designed us to be capable of going all in. And yet, gracious God that He is, He always lets us make the choice, though He won't always withhold consequence. But even in the tough love He counsels us to

> He breathes vitality in dead spaces and offers His marvelous, illuminating light in places that are dark.

choose the better way. "Those who love their life in this world will lose it. Those who care nothing for their life in this world will keep it for eternity" (John 12:25).

Yes, wanting God more requires something of us.

But thanks be to God, it is not the end of the story.

Because wanting God fulfills, completes…

Revives.

And that is the other part to the *what do you want?* question.

And oh…it's good.

Because when God brings revival, He brings Himself.

Travels (of the Few)

Some of us—a very few—will get the Jesus we say we want in this way…we who will embody the humility of John and become only the watermark in our own lives—present, but fading into the background of Him. When we ask God to come to the foreground of our lives, to move us in a vibrant way of revival, we must be willing to be moved.

> We can't want our life and want God at the same time.

When the Supernatural blows on us, it blows our status quo away. His Spirit dances in a freestyle way that knows nothing of a safe, typical, or manageable rhythm. And then we who want God more than anything else will be swept up in a tornado of transformation.

I admit that when I was younger, I let my tongue run loose with words to God—words like *I want You* and *I need You* and *I am willing to change, no matter what it takes.* But one day in my early twenties, on the floor of an out-of-town hotel room, I prayed such words on bended knee beside my sweet mother, and I discovered that He took them literally. I saw my *whatever it takes* prayer answered in the form of loss and pain and years of struggle, as I recount in my book *{w}hole.*

And though I have since prayed those words again, I have never prayed them as easily.

I want to make this easy on us because that feels so much better, but the truth is, when we pray for our own soul's revival we pray for *upheaval*. We are frail and scare easily, and God is gracious to not reveal all His plans or define what *upheaval* means. In our finiteness we would quake at the scale of them.

When we want God more than anything, we forgo our control of what life looks like. We must be ready for popularity lost. Comfort interrupted. Reason tossed away. Self disregarded. Sin exposed.

We have to welcome mountains to move. Not the mountains in glossy scenery books but the rugged, formidable kind that leave us reliant on a compass. The mountains so high we lose our breath. The mountains that bring out our primal instinct and expose our fingernails packed with dirt as we have tried to clutch it on our ascent into His world of *more*. Wanting God births such untamed things.

And I suspect that this, my friend, scary as it sounds, may also get your blood pumping. We were born to live on the edge and when someone reminds us it is possible, our heart responds.

> Wanting God births such untamed things.

And still we're scared. I marvel at mountains moving, yet the idea of taking up my cross daily (Luke 9:23) feels too heavy. I know it will require sweat and guts and may leave splinters. My heart screams, *Please just let me be!* and *Let me have God, too*. I want Him on the silver platter and unleashed to move radically in me at the same time. It is the rub of all humankind.

Where there is change there will first be a denial of something that hasn't worked and a newfound focus and effort on something that *will*. And where there is such effort there will only be a few.

This thought doesn't come from me, for I would hope for a broader opening, a wider road, guaranteeing a shot to more travelers. But I read Isaiah 35, which tells of the travels of the few willing, gutsy ones. They follow God and will one day enjoy peace and goodness in places that were dark. Though this passage is about the time when the earth as we know it will be no more, it makes me think about the road we can still walk to being spiritually revived, transformed, likened to God today.

> And a great road will go through that once deserted land.
> It will be named the Highway of Holiness…It will be only
> for those who walk in God's ways…Only the redeemed
> will walk on it (Isaiah 35:8-9).

I can try to make God smaller, but it will not change His greatness. I can paint the road to my soul's revival smoother, but it will not change the fact that it will likely have potholes and rocks. Wanting God is wanting more than what I can know, see, feel, or understand. It is being willing to travel the present-day Highway of Holiness, which is sure to be narrow and windy and complicated and long and messy.

> Wanting God is wanting more than what I can know, see, feel, or understand.

Most of us bail when the revival fires nip closer to our heels and the prayers for *whatever it takes* are taken seriously. We have only given half our hearts, gone partway in, and we are scared. But those who choose it will see the impossible become what only God makes possible.

Deserts will grow flowers.
Bad knees will become well.
Blind eyes will see.
Broken bodies will leap like deer.

Water will spring up in dry places (Isaiah 35:1-7).

These are promises for our future and spiritual promises for today. They are promises for everyday people who want God more than anything else and are willing to let Him bust up their ordinary lives for glimpses of the radical.

Travels of the few.

People like Florrie Evans.

Revival

> Revive deep spirituality in my heart; Let me live near to the great Shepherd, hear his voice, know its tones, follow its calls.*

I put her in a long dress and make her out to be uncomfortable. This picture painted in my mind, of her cursing the long, hot dress under her breath as she enters the church, lets me feel like she could be me. She feels *human.* She is no saint, greater or more spiritual than others, but she comes to the worship place today wanting God. On that single premise, I can relate.

It's 1904 and Valentine's Day in Wales. The imprint of the Great One is fresh on Florrie's teenaged heart, as she has only recently come to know Him. She is tender. Awake. Naïve to the rules of the pew. Unaware that she need be religious. Florrie is the embryo, the seed, the fetus undisturbed in quiet water that only knows of goodness— the way we all are when we first meet God and haven't yet had our faith tarnished.

She sits without thought to her sitting and listens without skepticism, two things most longtime churchgoers cannot do. She is all

---

* Arthur Bennett, ed., *The Valley of Vision: A Collection of Puritan Prayers and Devotions* (Carlisle, PA: The Banner of Truth Trust, 1975).

in with the message when, without her permission, the hinges of her heart become loose and rattled as the Spirit's Rushing Wind blows in. Furious. Hard, fast, and reverberating, like a whistling train with hot wheels on the tracks, He is whispering breathy commands to the deep-down place of courage. The commands push aside the thoughts that repeat, like a broken record, *sit still* and *stay quiet* and *you are too young, a woman, and no one will listen to you.*

And before she can stuff herself back into her skin, her legs stand tall and her mouth opens to say seven words that change everything.

"I love Jesus with all my heart."

I picture her shaking. She feels the fear in her fingertips while her heart still burns with courage. She has turned her soul inside out in front of God and everyone, and it is only because the love exceeds the fear that she can stand. It is always loving God more than other things that makes us brave.

God knows it is often the small one who inspires the great many. It is not the visible or famous but the everyday, blue-collar David with a pebble who slays a giant; the outcast with a pot no one wants to drink from who provides the Great I AM with water; the boy with a few fish who provides enough to feed thousands of people until they burp. But that's how grassroots Jesus movements happen.

> It is always loving God more than other things that makes us brave.

And the revival that has already swept into Florrie's soul now sweeps through the church in which she stands, cutting through jaded hearts of convenience and schedule and *don't call me, I'll call you* attitudes toward God. And people twist in their seats and wetness starts to form in eyes and the Rushing Wind blows hard and strong and the place begins to feel His rattling. A young woman wanting God most professed Him with lips and heart. Many say it is one of the main catalysts of how Jesus changed people in the Welsh Revival.

And oh, that God would do that again, today in you and in me—everyday, imperfect, unfulfilled, baggage-carrying people! Our minds can hardly contain the thought. Could He, would He, *will* He?

As we are inspired by the testimony of true revival, we tremble, yet we allow our hearts to *expect*. And for those of us who have decided that revival is truly what we want, we whisper this prayer under our breath:

Oh God, use me, too.

Bring my soul revival.

Bring me the epic *and the* extraordinary *and the* amazing *and the* never before.

Bring me awakening and anguish and fullness and joy that exceeds human understanding.

Bring change. Make me different. Rock me to my core. Help me never be the same.

Bring me You, God. I want You.

And despite our humanity and flaws and all, heaven hears.

Know What You Want

I ask, purposefully again and for the last time in this chapter, *What do you want?*

If it is life as we know it that we want, that can be ours. It is what we already have and already know—and we hang on to it even when it fails us.

When we are young, we do not yet know about bodies that grow weak and betray us. We do not know about weak knees and feet that can no longer run. We do not know about minds that cannot hold on to memories. The older I get the more clearly I see this, as life on earth is not meant to be kept, but lost, and this seeming cruelty of loss is, indeed, simply the process.

This life is all we know. We haven't seen the *promised,* so we don't know how astounding it is. We just know the love of family, the brush of summer sun on our cheeks, colors of flowers we snap in pictures since they are too pretty to put into words. We know the way it feels to worship Him with others in loud song and to birth babies and ideas and discover our gifts and our art. But we don't know the good life, the real life yet. We can't, because we are still here on earth.

But before we allow that to excuse us from living fully and passionately and boldly and well, we must remember that Jesus created us to stay here awhile and squeeze the most out of it—the most joy, the most faith, the most love, the most service. He set us up to have the *more* life in the temporal life…the one where we are born, thriving, and die, withering on the outside while we move closer to completeness. We lose everything we are told to clutch but stay with Jesus and win in the end. This is true life. This is wanting more and having it.

What do you want? He doesn't just ask the quick-to-follow disciples in John 1. He asks the question again in John 5, speaking to a limp-bodied man lying next to the healing waters of a pool he is too weak to enter. Jesus asks it not only to remind this man that he cannot heal himself, but also to prompt the man to dive into his own beliefs and hopes and desires to truly have a thriving life. He asks it of Peter in John 21, saying, "Do you love me more?" Jesus Christ, the greatest Counselor of all time, knew what every good counselor knows: They need only ask us the right question to get us to go to the core of who we are.

It is what He asks of us today, friend—in the gentle nudges in the pages of this book and in the moments that come long after the last page has been read and the cover has been shut. If we want Him in a way that literally nothing else matters, wearing desperation and passion in heart and on skin, we can indeed have Him. And how our life will be richer for it! But we have to be tired of our usual life. We have to be tired of getting up every day and seeing the car and the house in the suburbs and *still* not being fulfilled. We have to be tired of an adequate but stale-as-the-bread-in-our-kitchen relationship with God—a relationship that we have tried and tried to resuscitate and jumpstart by ourselves.

We can even know we need it. But until we want, that need will never be met. We have to want God not in the temporary or partial, but in the permanent and full. And I know, because I am about as human as you can get, that this sounds super big and hard. That it sounds disruptive of our life as we now know it and may require things we don't like. But God is *good*. For everything we give up, we gain the more we *really* want deep down. Wanting more really just means that what we have now will no longer do, and we believe He has better.

I speak this message to a church in Tennessee for the very first time. It is a beautiful two-day gathering with all the usual touches that scream *women's event at a big church*—meaningful dramas, worshipful music, and T-shirts that are mostly just good for sleeping in. But this time, I am drawn to the shirt the women's ministry coordinator has created. On the front is the name of the weekend theme. But on the back is this phrase, and it has me at hello:

> Wanting more really just means that what we have now will no longer do, and we believe He has better.

I know what I want.

It's simple. It's five words, for goodness sake. But it's good. It's very, very good. The weekend has not yet officially begun but I am thinking of almost nothing else but what it would be like to go through life knowing what we really want.

I think we're bad at this, really. Women are, for sure. We are asked by our dinner date where we want to eat and we answer "I don't know" because we can't choose between Chinese and Mexican. We don't know what we want to eat and we don't know what we want to wear. We stand for hours in the closet, looking for the perfect thing to jump out at us and fling itself on our body so we won't have to choose. We have so many choices that we're paralyzed by indecision. It's as if we have so much we've lost our minds.

We don't know if we want a life of highs and lows with risk or a life of steady, predictable outcomes. We don't know if we would rather live in peace with a few friends or open ourselves up to a wider community and possibly, future wounds. We don't know if we want a passionate life with God or a measurable, fun-for-now life without Him. There are so many options that most of us waste our lives away wishing we could have it all.

But what if we did know? What if we settled this issue once and for all and never looked back? What if we could go through life steady and unwavering? What if we never again tried to fill our hearts and lives with things that don't matter and leave us empty and crying out to God once again? Here's something beautiful: We *can*.

We're not the first ones to fill our hearts and lives with other things. It's been going on for a long time. It's in our history. And the problem of it not fulfilling us? That's been around a long time too. Back around 520 B.C., during the reign of King Darius, God sends a message to the Jews through the prophet Haggai. He has noticed that the assignment he gave them 15 years earlier to finish the temple in Jerusalem has not yet been fulfilled. In the middle of their building project, they have begun slipping the contractors' phone numbers in their pockets, calling them after hours to build a nice house for them on the side. And as they have gotten more and more into their own projects, they have gotten less and less focused on God's. So God chooses Haggai to confront them.

> Why are you living in luxurious houses while my house lies in ruins? This is what the LORD of Heaven's Armies says: Look at what's happening to you! You have planted much but harvest little. You eat but are not satisfied. You drink but are still thirsty. You put on clothes but cannot keep warm. Your wages disappear as though you were putting them in pockets filled with holes! (Haggai 1:4-6).

Pockets filled with holes. What a word picture! God is basically saying here, "Hey, how is doing your own thing going for you? How is that eating a lot, drinking a lot, shopping a lot, making a lot of money thing working out? It's what you wanted, right?"

The eating a lot, drinking a lot, shopping a lot, making a lot of money thing didn't work out for them, and it's not working out very well for us, either. We are more depressed than we've ever been, more reckless than we've ever been, less satisfied than we've ever been, and hurting more, too. We have been so busy creating castles for ourselves that we haven't stopped to notice they aren't really very beautiful. And then we are surprised when the beauty queen, the rich person, the Hollywood star takes their own life? No one ever has it all when they build it for themselves.

It is time to know what we want. It is time to stop chasing the temporary in place of the eternal. It is time to stop putting wages in our pockets only to have them exit through the holes. It is time to come back to God, beg Him for revival, and start moving forward into the *most* and *best* that can be ours.

The Greater Desire

I don't expect us to go out in the yard and do spirit cheers and high kicks over the idea that if we choose to follow hard after God we might have to face some inconvenience. That is why we must want this with our entire heart and not just know in our head we need it. We can be told a million times over that we should want God, but our flesh will convince us every time it is a lie. So it then comes down to the ache and the longing of *what we want most*.

I call this *the greater desire*. Keep reading, because I have some important stories in the following chapters to illustrate this point and help you recognize it in your own life. But the greater desire is always about the trump card. It's the *I can pick this, but ooh, this is even better.* It's not about the lack of something, because most of us don't lack very much in the physical sense. It is about choosing the better thing, the richer thing, the more satisfying thing, the greater thing for every day in our future.

Sometimes we will want to kick a habit, like eating, shopping, smoking, cussing, lying, gambling…but until we are able to see what those habits have taken from us, we will not hate them enough to let them go. But our hatred can keep us tied to them, even after we've kicked them to the curb. So it has to be about something even bigger—something that has our attention and focus more than those other things do. It has to be about the greater desire, which, when it comes to God, appeals to our spirit, not our flesh. The principle of the greater desire says this:

> *I want to be well and whole more than I want to be tied to something that brings me down.*

> *I want to be alive in spirit more than I want to just make it through the day.*

I want God to consume me more than the mess that is currently consuming my life.

I want God to use me more than I want Him to use someone else who is more willing.

And when we can say these things, the greater desire for *more* will win.

Get in the Game

We start to die when we settle into our life. What I'm talking about is not the settling of personal acceptance, growing up, and gaining wisdom that helps us no longer be interested in the claw-and-scratch positional jockeying of life. That's healthy and in many ways, spiritual progression. We are at our very best when we make peace with who God made us to be.

When I say *we start to die* what I mean is that we stop the spiritually active part of living. We pretend things with God are okay when they are not. We ignore the nagging convictions to do or not do certain things because what is in front of us in the moment feels really good. We rest on the comfortable, the safe, the popular to get us through each day, even while that normalcy has its hands on our neck, strangling us.

Oh, we don't like this, but it's true: We can't serve God fully while we are all settled in, because God is the great unsettler. And He no more cares about our cushy comfort level than three-year-olds care about anything but themselves. He is in the business of taking a wrecking ball to our structured, settled existence because He knows that is what it will take for us to come alive.

> We can't serve God fully while we are all settled in, because God is the great unsettler.

The apostle John tells a familiar story that I mentioned briefly a few pages ago, but I want to revisit it and look at it closer here. First, the backstory.

Jesus has just performed a miracle, and He is now returning to Jerusalem for one of the Jewish holy days. There is a pool right inside the city, which I imagine to be as noticeable as a blinking road sign. It is surrounded by five covered porches you surely cannot miss.

A man is lying there who has been sick for a long time. Nearly four decades. He is quite settled, to say the least, waiting by the pool in his spot, his space. He can't get up. We don't know exactly what hinders him, but from Jesus's command to get up and walk, we can assume it is something that involves his legs not working.

Jesus asks him if he wants to get well—which, if it were me and I were having a bad day, would have me hurling a pool toy at His head. And yet Jesus Christ, the Great Counselor, knows how to ask the right question—a question that plunges to the core of who the man is to show him he cannot heal himself. It is interesting how the handicapped man makes it about the pool lamenting the fact that it is of no help to him when the One who can actually heal him is standing right there. And I wonder: How many times have we looked to someone or something for a solution, made it about something else, when the One we need most is right in front of us the whole time, ready to help?

But God knew. He saw. He came. He helped. He responded, just as He does to us in our sedentary, seemingly hopeless, helpless moments in life. This man couldn't make it without God. We can't make it without Him, either.

The issue of this man's physical condition was legitimately causing him to settle in. I can barely picture the scene without tears—the man trying to drag his limp body into the pool over and over again as others cut off his path, pushing their way in first. What choice did he have, when he could not move? And yet even in his limitations God had a purpose. Even in his state, God wanted to use his life.

God wants to use us too, even when we feel we give Him little to work with. It is not for us to decide whether He can use us, even though we constantly try to make that decision.

I'm not experienced enough, we say.

I'm tainted.

I'm not special enough.

I don't have that thing *others do.*

I can't speak well.

I don't stand out.

I wonder how often God wants to look at us and say, "Hey, thanks for weighing in, but how about I make that decision?"

Settling in happens when we believe that what we know now is what we will always know; who we are now is who we will always be. It is a mind-set, a belief system. We think that after 38 years of lying by our own sick pool, we are never going to be able to move. The truth is, some of us have been sick with grief, sick with fear, sick with insecurity, sick with self-loathing, sick with pride, sick with selfishness, sick with heart wounds for a very long time. And it's caused us to settle for a life that does not know *more*.

Jesus does not want us to stay stuck. He doesn't want us to let our memories, choices, or mind-sets hold us down. He wants to hear our heart and know of our deep needs. And then He wants us to move emotionally, spiritually, and yes, often physically from wherever we are. He wants us to get past ourselves, work with whatever we have, seek Him passionately, and with whatever bundle of mess we are, just get in the game.

That's what it means to say He requires something of us.

I know this because not that long ago, He reminded me.

As I mentioned in this book's introduction, I spent the first three months after my book *{w}hole* released picking emotional shrapnel out of my skin. It was a beautiful book to write, but sharing so deeply— sharing pieces of myself that had stayed dormant for nearly 20 years— left me affected.

The book had taken its toll on me, and one day I am feeling that kind of down that leads even strong people to sit in a dark room and close the blinds. I tell my husband this in the front seat of the car, road tripping with our family over Christmas. The kids, in a convenience store sugar coma and with new headphones on their ears pumping out music, are thankfully unaware.

"I want to quit, Scotty," I say to the right side of his face. He keeps driving, with the *I'm listening* look, but my emotions make me read it wrong and I'm convinced he needs me to repeat it. "I'm serious, Scotty. I am going to quit. I'm going to stop writing and stop speaking and yeah, even shut down my blog! What do you think of that?" We have been married for years so he is savvy to certain things at this point, like what happens when your wife really doesn't want you to agree with her but pretends she does because in that moment if you don't, it will make her mad. Yeah, *that*.

After what seems like hours, Scotty finally speaks, but there is no long speech. He doesn't so much as turn his face. "Okay. But why?"

Were I not so enraged by the fact he is not matching my passion, I would give him props for playing me just like I need to be played: calm, cool, without jumping into "fix-it man mode," asking a good question to get me to go to my core and dig deep.

I answer in the most honest way I know how: "I just want to be a normal person." And with that I am swallowed up, alone again, in my thoughts. *What does normal even mean? Do I want God to leave me alone and let me do what I want? Yes, yes, that's what I mean. I want God to leave me alone. It's too hard, pouring my guts onto pages of books and standing on stages being vulnerable about my junk. I want to worry about what color bow to put in my daughter's hair or which yoga pants to wear today or what is the next place our family can all go on vacation. I just want to be normal.*

With the silence of the car only being interrupted by a few occasional *Mom, how long until we get theres,* I am pouting. Thankfully, Scotty has left me alone, which only makes me love him more and simultaneously makes me furious. (I have no idea why in the world this man might find me complicated.) *He thinks I should quit,* I think to myself. *See, I was right.*

We get to our destination and are ushered into the swell of hugs and *I've missed yous* from friends in our past. It is so good to see them, so good to be somewhere besides in my head. We are set to go to dinner and I'm glad, because food will surely be my healer. Amid a rumbling of protests and great gnashing of teeth, we load our kids back into the car to head to the restaurant. After the long trip, they are not excited about spending another minute on the road.

We arrive at a place that boasts GOOD FOOD, GREAT TIMES on its wall, and I believe it. People are laughing. They are dancing to really loud music. They are having a good time, and I am happy for them. I want to have a good time too.

But I am not who I used to be. Having a good time used to mean losing my mind and living reckless. But now I am a mother. I am a wife. I am a woman whom God picked up from a dark place, brushed off, and infected with Himself. I cannot stop thinking about God. I'm frustrated with Him, but still, He consumes me.

I'm frustrated because I am a runner and He is not letting me run. I am a bailer, and I am stubborn. I do not want to be told I cannot quit when every inch of me wants to throw in the towel and go live a quiet life where I do what I want and serve God on my terms. *Oh, God,* is all I can say to myself, half in prayer, half in exasperation. *Food and music,*

Lisa, I think to myself. *For tonight, just food and music.* I am purposely trying to wipe Jesus out of my mind.

We sit at a long table with a clear view of the middle of the room. I find myself happy that the music will drown out conversation, for I am not in the mood to paste on a smile and pretend I am happy when all I really want to do is just be my own version of normal. It doesn't take us long to order or get our food. Before I know it, we have eaten, the table has been cleared, and we are middle-aged observers with coffee cups in our hands, watching the dance floor while our kids have become one with their phones and iPods.

I am enjoying the loud '80s music, even shoulder dancing a bit in my seat, when I notice the blonde woman with skinny legs. She is more than asking for all eyes to be on her. With her body language, she is flat-out demanding it. I size her up silently and deem her *that woman who still wants to be young and have all the attention like she used to,* which is not nice on my part. She's dancing now, wildly, in the middle of the room, with skinny legs flying and eyes that ask you to join in. I am drawn to the moment, to her eyes, to the music, to the whole thing.

And as I sit, drawn in, the Spirit butts in to do His own drawing. I do not look for Him or ask for Him, but He speaks anyway, straight and loud, without needing my permission.

So you want to be a normal person, Lisa?

I am frozen, ruminating on the moment, watching this woman before me and all of her dancing comrades. I hear their glasses clinking and the sound of beer taps flowing and laughter of the loud, cackling kind that usually goes with off-color jokes and flirting between strangers and stories that probably weren't supposed to be told but have been shared anyway.

And cutting through the whole scene are His words, His question: *So you want to be a normal person?* They are clear; there is no wiggling free from them. They have been dropped like a bowling ball onto my chest and I am quite sure I have stopped breathing. I cannot believe that even in my mess of a mind and above the loud moment, He has made His way to me. There is nowhere to run, nowhere to hide. I have been found.

I get it, what He says. I hear Him, loud and clear. I do not answer because I do not need to; He has made His point. But He does not stop speaking, for He is not through. He has more *bowling ball to the chest* words to say.

My people have fallen asleep, Lisa.

I need you in the game.

Get in the game.

And suddenly the room around me, once alive with carefree sounds of party happiness, turns into a quiet sanctuary. I am not in a raucous restaurant but back at that old summer camp where I'm sitting on a log with my pink Bible and it's all about me and God. He has romanced me, pulled me back in, given me tough love, inspired me to be better as only He can. I am, in that moment, determined, jolted, awakened, *back in the game.*

It's not a real game God plays with us. He won't play hide and seek or cat and mouse. *God doesn't play games.* But He doesn't want us to settle for sitting on the sidelines and watching our influence go by when He has given us the ability to play ball. He wants us to stop pouting, stop excusing, stop lamenting, stop rationalizing, and stop spending huge clumps of time reading self-help books and trying out strategies to fix ourselves and become our version of perfect before we decide He can use us. He needs us, now, to affect the world. He wants to use us now, where we sit.

I am a huge proponent of seeking counsel, becoming introspective, getting whole and well. We will have far cleaner vessels to serve Him when we have done the work, owned our stuff, and dealt with our baggage. But at some point, the process of fixing ourselves has to stop. We have to freefall into trust and not be afraid to just wear the stained

T-shirt to the party. We just have to show up. Many times change happens just by doing something different. Because the more we taste how sweet the living *more* with God is, the more we want it.

People who live all out for God aren't more special. They just tasted something good and kept going back for it. They just got in the game from whatever point they were. That's true progress. That's stepping out of the *okay* into the *more*. That's no longer fantasizing about being normal. That's finding the pinnacle of life—the *more* of heaven coming down to earth—while we still live here.

Remembering, Again

Please don't be intimidated by this idea of wanting more. It is why I write this book: to help you. I make you this promise: If you stay with me, I will tell you everything I know about having a dynamic, vibrant relationship with God and what gets in the way. Period. There will be no gimmicks or me pontificating my own wisdom or sharing with you all my success stories (since that would be a short book). But we will depend on Scripture and history to learn about the things that create movement with God. And like Florrie Evans, I want you to experience the Welsh Revival—your own personal revival—right at home, right where you sit, where you drink your coffee, make school lunches, drive to work, wherever. It is possible, and doesn't that bring hope?

> He needs us, now, to affect the world. He wants to use us now, where we sit.

I purposely got very serious with you early on in this chapter because I think we need to know the core, bottom-line truth about what this *more* journey looks like, and God deserves nothing less than for us to take it seriously and dive in all the way. We have enough stirred believers in the church who never take the journey beyond a stirring, and that is a spiritual waste.

And the first step on this journey? Remembering.

It's like the married couple who is feeling distant and pulls out their wedding video. As they watch it, the distance begins to melt. They find themselves being drawn in again to the love and to the promise and to *the one.* In the same way, we who are in a spiritual drought and need a reminder must revisit things too. We need to remember why we fell in love with God in the first place. And when we do the love wells and the desire grows and we remember why we are wanting *more.*

I meet a man at a rehab center who does this for me—helps me remember. The center, an old, stately home in a true town of nowhere, is so remote that even a long plane ride doesn't get me there. A nice lady who drives slower than any granny picks me up and drives me another hour to a place where the good people of the church feed me, and after the last bite I am whisked away to become this night's rehab center teacher. As I enter the home-turned-healing-place where addicts of all forms live, my ears are met with what can only be described as guttural moaning coming from the worship center. I am curious, but I don't have much time to think about it before I round the corner to see the source: a man holding a guitar. He is writhing, rocking, tapping, sway-ing, making his own version of a joyful noise. "I have decided to fol-low Jesus," he sings loudly, and I believe him because his countenance cannot lie. I do not know what this man has been delivered from, but it is clear to me that it is likely not small. I find myself wishing for ten minutes alone with him to hear the whole Jesus story. I want to know what the Rescuer pulled him out of because I know that whatever it is, it has produced within him an expression of gratitude like I have never before heard. In my flesh, I feel jealous of his obvious intimacy with God.

And as I listen to a man emoting to his Master, I think about my own life and how sometimes I forget to moan from my gut over God. I think about my casualness with Him, how life takes over and how somehow, on the pages of my journey, I have traveled far enough to become this groaning man's teacher for the night.

I think of passion plays and light blue padded pews and a child-hood friend named Kathy saying words to Jesus she doesn't mean. I think of the Jesus I met that night and how I chased Him down with little girl arms pumping and heart racing, feeling the bravest I'd ever felt in my entire life.

I remember what it feels like to come with open hands and heart and I am, again, awed by the Story of *in the beginning, water into wine, love held by nails, the veil torn, resurrected life.* He is real, more real than anything I will ever see with my eyes, hear with my ears, or touch with my hands.

I remember the power and the commitment. The beauty and the magnitude. The promises, the relationship, the raw passion for the cause and the reason and the immaculate, saving grace.

And I, the teacher, feel small, entitled, and forgetful. I feel jarred and sparked and raw. I want to sit longer in this place so I can have more of this glossed-down, minimalistic faith. I want to moan from my gut that I need God without caring who hears. I want to remember who He is and why I loved Him in the first place. I want God more than I did when I walked in, and this man's primal cries for *more* have been the cause.

I want to know Him and touch Him and never hurt His heart.

I want to love Him and feel His love back.

I want to talk to Him with the simple words I know.

I want to be casual about other things, but never about Him on a cross.

I want to tell God I want Him and I want to mean it.

I want God like I did the first time, and it consumes every grown-up square inch of me.

And right before I take the stage and become the teacher, I cry, like all of us who have forgotten and then remembered again do.

2

I Want God
More Than Comfort

*There are risks and costs to action. But they are far less
than the long-range risks of comfortable inaction.*

JOHN F. KENNEDY

Until recently, when health magazines kept preaching to me about
the dangers of diet drinks and I had a dream I was a lab rat who
was dropper-fed so much soda I got cancer and I all but quit one day
cold turkey, you could find me on any given morning with a left hand
of cold and a right hand of hot: soda with a side of coffee.

I liked it for breakfast. I liked it in my car, taking up both cup
holders.

It is where I am some months ago when my oldest son in the pas-
senger seat next to me (he's at the age where he speaks up about most
things) decides to playfully confront me about my hot and cold pref-
erences and the fact they include a heated seat for my backside with air
conditioning cooling off my face.

"Mom?" he says. "You don't make sense to
me. Why would you want your seat warm
but cold air blowing on you at the same
time? Isn't that kind of a contradiction?"

I smile, the sheepish kind, and answer
him honestly, but before I can really think.

Bottom Line

When comfort is your
immediate priority,
God cannot move.

45

"Well, son, I guess I just like to be comfortable."

He smiles back, shakes his head, playfully, and I feel silly. What I said was true. It just sounds so *Beverly Hills Housewives* to say it.

Things about comfort, things that are true but we don't like to say, go further than that. When it comes to spiritual things, it is hard for most of us to be completely honest about what has kept us from God because when we say them out loud they, too, sound silly, like contradictions.

The comfort I enjoy is what ultimately keeps me from God, for whom my heart groans.

When I over-insulate it nullifies God's plan for me to feel the chill of being without and needing Him to be the only one who can take care of that problem.

I desperately want God to use me, but instead I choose to be comfortable, which never supports that core passion.

There's a trade-off, see. The quick fix good news is that we can be warm if we want. We can find a way to cover ourselves so tightly that cold reality can't hit us and we stay insulated, shielded on our terms, *comfortable.*

But insulation in the spiritual doesn't create true or long-term warmth.

It just creates *immobility.*

This I experience physically two family Christmas trips ago.

I am in my room packing for a trip our family of five will take to the mountains to go snow tubing, our first tubing trip as a family. As I stuff sweater after sweater into my suitcase, husband-borrowed long johns, wool socks I wouldn't normally wear because they would crowd most regular shoes, I have one mantra in mind: *I will not be cold.*

I am proud of my grand packing plan, which has me dreaming of our vacation. In it, I visit this nearby mountain with my people, more than prepared. In full snow armor I step out with warm boots onto beautiful white powder, laugh at the swirling, icy air around me and like a snow ninja, beat my hands on my fluffy-coated chest and shout over and over, loudly, *Haha! I'm warm!* and never feel a thing. This is my goal for me. It is my goal, too, for my people.

A few days later, we arrive at our snow tubing destination. I step with warm boots onto beautiful white powder, excited to snow tube with my family. I am covered head to toe, including the black ski mask on my face I purchased at the last minute which no one has the heart to tell me makes me look crazy.

(Ski burglar? *Yes.* Cold ski burglar? *No.*)

I am proud. I, the snow ninja, have reached my goal: The cold can't touch me. My mission to feel absolutely nothing on this wintry, cold day has been accomplished.

There is only one problem.

In all of my insulated layers, I cannot move. Literally, full on *can't.* And suddenly my grand plan doesn't feel so grand.

My mission to feel no cold has been accomplished. But my greater desire* to enjoy snow tubing with my family has been inadvertently thwarted by my self-inflicted immobility.

By my own doing and my desire to not be cold, I have made myself immobile and sabotaged my joy.

This is what comfort does to us: It sabotages the things we really want. Future, dreams, peace, fulfillment, spiritual mobility, *joy.* We become enslaved by its rules.

And now, if I'm being that level of truthful that's felt in the gut, I must admit the depth of my immobility.

I live for comfort. I eat it, breathe it, sleep

> Insulation in the spiritual doesn't create true or long-term warmth.

---

* Remember this phrase from Chapter 1?

it, with exactly two pillows of varying softness perfectly made to stack on each other to prove it.

I want a bath when I want a bath.

I want ice in my drink, but not too much so it sticks together and I barely get enough drink in the glass so I have to keep refilling. I want the perfect amount.

I want clean sheets on my bed without having to bend over and put them on myself.

I want restaurants to not be closed when I want to go to them and my car to never break down but always work to carry me where I go when I want to go there.

And this list could go on because there is no end to what this flesh I wear wants in order to feed its ugly monster of comfort.

I'm betting you have your list, too.

But if God is ever going to invade our insides and do that powerful work we groan for, we are going to have to stop sabotaging it by insulating ourselves to the point where neither He nor we can move.

The Issue of the Band-Aid

The reason we do not have more of God is that we make our immediate need for comfort the priority.

I call it the Issue of the Band-Aid. Let me explain.

When my son was young (but old enough to watch Band-Aid commercials), he wanted to use them on everything on his body that hurt. He got in the cabinet, found them even in the way back place I'd stuck them, and put them on places he wanted to feel better. He understood nothing about the healing process. He didn't know that Band-Aids are temporary solutions, not cures for ankles that are sprained or wounds that are deep. All he knew was that Band-Aids covered hurt. And he wanted immediate relief, so this became his perfect solution.

And we, people who get banged up, wounded, and scraped up by life, tend to reach for the Band-Aids, too. We want immediate relief from the empty existence we have created for ourselves and will comfort ourselves in any way that will make it possible. We will comfort ourselves with shopping. We will comfort ourselves with food. We will comfort ourselves with sex. We will comfort ourselves with porn. We will comfort ourselves with prescription drugs. We will comfort ourselves with TV. We will comfort ourselves with self-help conferences and keeping our calendar all booked up: Band-Aids that solve nothing and cannot heal our deep hurt.

We diminish the depth of the wound, applying topical solutions to deep-down things that need attention. We blame the porn for entangling us, the shopping for being accessible, the food for being so tempting, the drugs for being so addicting, when our desire to comfort ourselves has been the problem all along. We can't see it for what it is because the Band-Aid of temporary comfort is covering it—Band-Aids in the form of things and even people.

Things

A true story is written of a set of feuding brothers, twins so at odds that even before they are born they fight inside their mother's stomach. The rivalry is present at birth, as the younger comes out grasping the heel of the older like a toddler at preschool jockeying to be first in line. As they grow up they divide their household and parents. One brother is a wild outdoorsman, which pleases his father; the other is a mama's boy who likes to stay at home. The rivalry is present, still, as they become young men.

There comes a day when the mama's boy is cooking, and his wild outdoorsman twin comes in, hungry and tired from outdoor work. He smells the food and his mouth starts to water. He wants some, and he wants some now.

"I'm starved!" the older twin says. "Give me some of that red stew you've made."

But younger twin who is cooking is a clever one, and he will never just give the food to his brother in a gracious, brotherly kind of way. Instead, he will leverage, finding a way to make his brother's plight his advantage.

"All right, but trade me your birthright for it," stew-making mama's boy says. The request is not stew-worthy. It is far beyond. He is asking for an honor given only to the firstborn son—material wealth, the prestige of leadership one day when the patriarch passes on. It's a big deal that will last far longer than a bowl of soup. Yet mama's boy wants to trade.

Was it the desperation in his hungry brother's eyes that told him he would agree to the request? I wonder this about him, though I'll never know. Or did he put it out there, thinking, *He won't agree to it but it's worth a shot?* If he did, he sorely underestimated the power of comfort: how it convinces you to give up the better things for the things of right now. It is just what the older twin did.

As a result of this unequal trade, the older brother did in fact lose his blessing. His younger, craftier brother took advantage of his situation, offering him some comfort food to ease his present need. In a weak moment, without thinking of the future, the hungry sportsman brother took it. And the rest is history. (You can read the story yourself in Genesis 25.)

I find myself in the hungry sportsman brother. I have, at times, compromised the future for brief moments of comforting pleasure. I suspect you have too. We have caved to the thing that feels good for now but costs us big in the future—turned a blind eye to it because the *for now thing* yelled louder, promising it would make us full.

This is how comfort works. It feels warm and relaxing and pleasurable and unable to be done without. But it doesn't plan a future. We are blinded by the now, ruled by the flesh. As soon as the high wears off, we require another fix.

I've been reading the book of Job recently, and I'm struck by some amazing imagery in chapter 8 that I have previously overlooked. It is the response of Bildad, one of Job's three friends with whom he dialogues about his great suffering (lost wealth, family, and health). Job expresses his weariness over his situation and says he is wracking his brain to figure out God in it all. Though Bildad's response is both accusatory and assumptive about where Job must have gone wrong to incur such pain, what he writes in verses 13 and 14 is dead-on in regard to how the comfort we look for in things is unstable at best, ensnaring at worst.

> The same happens to all who forget God.
> The hopes of the godless evaporate.
> Their confidence hangs by a thread.
> They are leaning on a spider's web.

We might at first read this and feel we cannot relate. Most of us do not consider ourselves to be godless. We might have forgotten God some here and there in the business of life, but we still think of ourselves as pretty good. But what about counting on other things? Have we not done that? Have we not relied on things other than God only to have them collapse around us? Have we not put our faith in our jobs only to have them taken from us without our permission? Have we not relied upon relationships to complete us that have been less than fulfilling? Have we not leaned on things that didn't hold us, just like a spiderweb would do if we leaned against it?

If we're honest with ourselves, *yes*. My friend Kelly is honest with me about this, sitting in bare feet on the couch during our recent girls' trip. She's my childhood friend, one of my longest, the kind who knows the name of a junior high boyfriend. We've gone on this trip to have fun, yes, but also to heal. Kelly's felt loss a lot in the past few years, first with her beloved father dying, then with her oldest and only daughter getting married and leaving the home. Just two months earlier her son headed off to college, leaving her with an empty nest. It's been hard for her lately, and she needs to get away. We meet from our homes many states apart for a weekend life reprieve.

One night after sun and dinner, we ease into the living room to talk about her daddy and the hollow place left from his passing. I knew the man, Charlie, so I can picture his smile, quick words, and easy demeanor. I remember how his grins made me feel at ease and how Kelly adored him. She took his death hard, like all daddy's girls do.

She talks to me about how she has this necklace. It is a necklace her daddy gave her that she loves so much she never takes it off. It is the last thing he leaves with her when he leaves this earth—a token of his love that in some way makes her feel he is still with her. She wears it all the time, but wears it afraid—afraid that she will lose it, that the clasp will break and it will be gone and in that loss she will feel as though she's lost him again. Her friend knows this and offers something amazing: She will put it in a shadow box and preserve his gift forever. Kelly is thrilled at this offer and promptly puts it in a safe, padded envelope and mails it to her out-of-town friend.

A few weeks later, Kelly gets a phone call. It is her friend, the one who has offered her the sweet gift, whose voice sounds small and wavering. She holds her sobs in, but Kelly can tell she has been crying. "I don't know how to tell you this," her friend says, voice breaking, "but somehow I've lost your necklace."

Kelly is silent. She does not know what to say. She is thrashing about inside, replaying the words to try to believe them. *She's lost the necklace*, she thinks to herself. *She's lost that piece of him I still had that I love.* She wants to be angry and for the circumstance, she is. Her heart is sobbing, breaking over the reality that her daddy cannot give her another piece of himself, for he is gone. He cannot replace the necklace and neither can she, and this stings like a face in cold wind. But Kelly knows her friend is hurting and she knows, too, that making this thing more important than her friend's beautiful attempt at love is misplaced and wrong. It won't bring the necklace back, or her daddy. It will just be a relationship to be fractured, pain to be carried out in a different place. She is no saint, but she knows she must forgive and let go.

In a moment that looks like Jesus, Kelly offers her friend grace. She tells her she is not angry with her. She tells her not to carry the burden that is not hers to bear. She wants her to know she loves her, still.

As only God can do, He has provided for Kelly in her moment of pain a clear perspective: how this thing she has so dearly loved and has been clinging to for months is gone and so is her daddy, but He is not. She is aware anew that things will never be enough, never stick around every time we want them to, never hold us for the long haul. There will only be God. He will be the One left standing after all the things are gone. Something Kelly loves is gone. But she lives on for much more.

Things cost us, friends. Things can be our Band-Aids. They may cover places so we won't see them but they will ultimately solve nothing. Things keep us comfortable but comfort keeps us from God.

The food.

The porn.

The shopping.

The TV.

The house and car.

These are some of our comforts. They are our trophies and trinkets—the fuzzy dice we hang from the rearview mirror of our car. They are our cheap replacements for God.

When we are unwilling to forgo such comforts—the ones that feel good but ultimately keep us immobile and unfeeling, the ones that seem like a good idea at the time but in the end wind up costing us big—we say to God, *Comfort is better than You. What I want in this moment is worth forgoing what You offer long-term.*

Hedonism.

This is not a new problem.

It was a young rich guy's problem back in Jesus's time too. He's called "someone" in the Word, maybe because he could be any one of us at any given time who longs to hold onto the things in life that aren't meant to be kept. In his case, it was money. The rich kid's issue was that he liked it too much.

> Jesus told him, "If you want to be perfect, go and sell all your possessions and give the money to the poor, and you will have treasure in heaven. Then come, follow me."
>
> But when the young man heard this, he went away sad, for he had many possessions (Matthew 19:16-22).

This young man wanted God, but he wanted things more. He was stuck on money, settled in his comfort of wealth. He asked the right questions and showed interest in the eternal but when it came down to it, he held onto the thing that was familiar and safe, even though it would mean he would spend an eternity apart from God.

A costly contradiction.

We read this and can't fathom it.

But we have done it, too.

People

> Man's desire for God is bedded in his unconscious and seeks to satisfy itself in physical possession of another human. This necessarily is a passing, fading attachment in its sensuous aspects since it is a poor substitute for what the unconscious is after.*

---

* Flannery O'Connor, *A Prayer Journal* (New York: Farrar, Straus and Giroux, 2013), 30.

In a comfort-driven world, people can easily double for Band-Aids. We take comfort in companionship, a listening ear, empathetic hugs, and words of affirmation. People make us feel better. They tell us there is good in us when we are sure there is only bad. An amazing few friends dive into our mess with us, help us sort it out, and make us feel safe in the process. It's why God meant for us to have people to travel with in life—to be His hands and feet on earth and help each other both thrive and endure. He just never meant for any of us to take the place of Him.

But leave it to our flesh, and we will use them as Band-Aids. We will lay them over the issues that keep us from moving closer to God. We will focus on them, giving them our attention, sure they will meet our needs. We will turn to them in moments when our hearts hurt and we so badly want to talk to another person when what we need to do is talk to our Father. It's why God says in Jeremiah 33:3, "Call to me and I will answer you. I'll tell you marvelous and wondrous things that you could never figure out on your own" (MSG). Other people can't figure our life out for us. We can't either, without God.

And take a deep breath, friend, because it gets harder. For a die-hard family lover like me it stings to say this, but it's true: We have to choose God above everyone else, even our own family. There is no clause in the Word that says, "God comes first unless family is in the picture, in which case God can be second," or "God comes first unless you are in a relationship with a God-honoring person. That's enough to please God." No. It's not. Read Matthew 19:29—red-letter words straight from God's lips:

> And everyone who has given up houses or brothers or sisters or father or mother or children or property, for my sake, will receive a hundred times as much in return and will inherit eternal life.

Brothers, sisters, fathers, mothers, children—even *children*, people. And what God is saying here is not that He wants us to throw people away or treat our family poorly by not caring for them well, esteeming them, holding them with both hands as gifts. What He's saying is, "I have to be most valuable. I have to be most important. I have to be the greater desire over even your most treasured thing in life. Everyone else you can live without but Me. You have to want Me most, and wanting Me most means making Me more important than even your most beloved relationships."

Remember the rich young guy I just told you about in the last section? Interestingly, Jesus says the above words to His disciples right after He speaks to the rich kid and tells him to give up his stuff. He reminds everyone within earshot that following Jesus not only requires the giving up of things but of people, too. And most of the time, people are the harder sacrifice.

But He does not require this of us without going first. Even at the age of 12, He illustrates this principle of God over people when He takes a trip to the Temple with His parents but doesn't journey the miles back home with them. Instead, He stays in the Temple for the greater thing: to be the mouthpiece of God.

By so doing, what He does to His mother emotionally is a thing only we who are parents can know. How the sheer panic and fear of a lost son must have wrapped its tentacles around Mary's body when she realized He was missing! (If the way I felt when I lost my son in Target for five minutes that time when he was a toddler even comes close, she was in need of heavy sedation.)

> "Son," his mother said to him, "why have you done this to us? Your father and I have been frantic, searching for you everywhere" (Luke 2:48).

And then young Jesus—Jesus who does not raise His alarm to meet hers—lovingly but pointedly answers back, "But why did you need to search?…Didn't you know that I must be in my Father's house?" (Luke 2:49).

They should have known.

Young Jesus, living as flesh, separated from His parents in the travel, staying back without them and their comfort, couldn't have loved anyone more than His family…anyone except for God. He couldn't ignore His higher calling to His heavenly Father, which had Him doing the more important thing. The relationship with His parents? Trumped.

It's a tough one, I know. But friends, giving up people does not mean discarding them or considering them less valuable. It means people are second and God is first, something even our family must know.

I question this hard thing myself a few weeks ago, alone in a hotel room for a conference at which I am speaking. It is Friday night, and that seems sacrifice enough, since Friday night means football night for my varsity wide-receiver son. Sports and family…which on this night will not include me. My son has earned his starting spot as a sophomore, and I am proud of his hard work and hopeful that the many hours in the gym and many passes caught in practice will finally be rewarded with a touchdown, which has thus far eluded him. I want it for him because he wants it. But I also selfishly hope it will not happen during a weekend I am gone because I want to be there too.

Despite a myriad of mistakes I have made as a mom over the past 15 years, I've managed to rarely ever miss a thing, which makes me feel good. I haven't missed first steps or first teeth or first words. I haven't missed homecoming dances or first days of school or conversations over hot meals at dinner. I've been there for my children's firsts, even though I have traveled and spoken and at times been gone. God has so graciously worked it out better than I ever could have, and I feel like I have done what He's asked me to do without compromising my family in the process.

So it only made sense that I would be there when this milestone happened, too. And I would get to snap the picture and make a blessed fool out of myself as I screamed the loudest in the stands. I would be around to see that grin with dimples I live for and get to wrap my arms around a smelly, padded jersey and then pull back and look into my firstborn's eyes and say, "Son! You did it!"

I am sitting on my hotel room bed, midway through sourdough bites and 20/20 on the TV when the first text comes in alerting me to the happenings of the game I am missing, giving me an inkling of what just might be to come.

"Lisa, your boy just caught a pass!"

My girlfriend, a football mom too, knows I am out of town, and that my husband is keeping team stats and is unlikely to keep me posted during the game. She knows I will want to know. So game to phone, phone to hotel room, blow by blow, she becomes my personal announcer throughout the game.

Caught up in the next texts coming in, I can hardly breathe. "He caught another one, Lisa!" "Oh, now he just caught a two-point conversion!" I have long abandoned my interest in the TV and have stopped eating the sourdough bites altogether. I'm living the moment through my football mom friend and though my heart is filled with joy for my son who I know is beside himself excited for the game's happenings, I am becoming increasingly aware I am missing it all. And it's starting to make me sad.

It is about this time I finally receive a text from my husband. It is the one I had both prayed for and hoped against, all at the same time. "Graham just scored a 47-yard touchdown!" The instinctive selfless mom part of me takes over and for this moment puts sulking mom in the corner, screams like a banshee with both arms thrown up in the air, tears coming down my cheeks, ringing the invisible cowbell, throwing the imaginary confetti. My son has scored his first touchdown, and I am sure this moment feels something like heaven.

But then, in the next moment, reality enters my brain. I am not in the stands ringing a cowbell, screaming like a banshee with arms raised high in the air, seeing that dimple when it comes to the sidelines and the helmet comes off. No, I am standing in a quiet hotel room, wearing yoga pants and eating sourdough bites from a welcome basket. My son scored his first touchdown, and I was not there to see it.

I'm grieved. I am not there for my son. I do not get to be a part of this important milestone in his life. Of all the games I am there for I miss this one, the one which counted the most. God willing, there will be more touchdowns. But there will never be this *first*. The understanding settles in and, standing in the middle of my hotel room, I start to cry.

"God," I say between tears, "why? Why this weekend? Why this game? Why me here and him there? You know I want to be a good mom and not miss anything. So why?"

Even in this moment, I feel a bit dramatic and silly. I know in my head this is *football*, not a cancer diagnosis or a car wreck or a kid-who-just-got-caught-with-drugs life moment. I know this is just one touchdown in a potential career of more, but it doesn't seem right to be penalized when I am somewhere speaking for God.

And then, in that way only He can, He gives me a silent heart-whisper that says, "It's a good thing you love Me more."

I'm sad and mad but deep down, I know He's right. It reminds me of something one of my spiritual heroes, missionary Elisabeth Elliot, said: "When obedience to God contradicts what I think will give me pleasure, let me ask myself if I love Him." I don't want this statement to ring in my ears or for it to apply to this situation or, if I'm painfully honest, for God to even ask me to love Him more. I hear His statement more as a question, and even in the moment I am forced to take inventory. Do I love Him more? Do I want to go where He asks me to go if it means I have to sacrifice an important experience with my child, whom I love more than my very own life? And if He asks me to give up this, what more might He ask me to give up that I don't want to? It is as if I know there are bigger things He might ask me to give up next.

I *want* to love Jesus more. I *believe* I love Jesus more. But many days, the theory isn't tested. He's asked me to give up things for Him and some of those things haven't been easy but He thus far hasn't asked me for people in my life I love. The moment is bigger than a missed football touchdown by my son. It's the realization, anew, that nothing, not even my children, can come before Him.

Friend, please hear me. This is not about chasing a goal or dream and in that selfish pursuit, leaving our children and families in the dust. God does not ordain human pursuits if they break down the structure of the home, for that would contradict His Word and character, which He cannot do. But will He ask for our sacrifice to reveal and facilitate our first loyalties to Him? Yes. And must we be willing to lay anything, anyone aside for that greater allegiance? Yes to that, too.

People can get in the way of God. They can be our go-to when it's supposed to be Him.

God wants His seat in our lives. Most of us have given it to someone else.

We may like the idea of wanting God more than any*thing* else, but when that comes to an any*one*—someone we can see, smell, and touch—we want to opt out. When it comes to breaking down what wanting God more really means, most of us don't like those realities because we realize it could mean *sacrifice.* It is no wonder, then, that we have not seen God move radically in our lives. We have never gotten to the place where we have fully released the comforts that hold us. We have, instead, held onto them.

The truth is, we will not change until we get to the point we are sickened by what our comfort has cost us.

It's cost us God.

Ticket Price

Comfort sells itself well, but its ticket price is expensive.

It has cost us in personal ways, though it seems like it is that ready friend, always doing us a favor. But it's a quick fix with no long-term benefits. With comfort, in the moment it's all good. But when that moment is over, another fix is needed.

It keeps us from figuring out who we really are

It is human nature to have go-to responses to things in our life we don't like.

We are hurt and we go to the comfort of staying busy so we don't have to deal with it.

We are lonely and we go to the comfort of casual sex.

We are mad and we go to the comfort of yelling angry words.

We are controlling and we go to the comfort of sticking our finger down our throat to throw up the food we just ate.

But these go-to comfort responses hurt us, because they keep us from finding out who we really are outside of them. They hurt us, solve nothing for us…but we run to them because they are at least familiar.

Yet it's a prison. Attached to our go-to responses of comfort, we can't feel the freedom on the other side of the fence. We won't experience honest, healthy emotions. We won't find and enjoy pure relationships.

Comfort lies to us. It cushions us from our own reality. It keeps us from seeing the places in our life that need to grow and change. It prevents us from figuring out who we really are and could be without the crutch. So while it feels good in the moment, ultimately, it imprisons us.

It costs us greater service

Comfort has us desiring the easier path, craving a normal life where we do not do anything too *out there* for God.

On some hard ministry days, having a normal life (whatever that is) sounds like a one-way trip to Fiji in one of those private huts over azure waters with a fruit smoothie in my hand, pajama pants all day, and nary a cell phone in sight. I would be lying if I said I haven't at times craved that normalcy. But every time I long to be comfortable, that greater desire to serve God moans louder until it gets my attention. Even when we ignore it, the God-call inside all of us does not keep quiet.

In everyday life, the God-call persists too. Many of us want to be comfortable and are able to achieve this for spans of time. We are able to ignore the global needs, the hurts of the homeless, the needs of the people who live next door to us but whose names we do not know. We are able to go on vacation, open shiny presents on Christmas, laugh at barbecues with friends while our nostrils drink in the smell of grilling, function in our own world with brief interactions with God being okay. But at some point this won't be enough. None of these things—none of anything that ever comforts us—will be enough.

This was God's plan: to create humans with the innate longing for Him. It is why, then, try as we may, we can't ever be satisfied a different way. It's why a half-in, vanilla Christianity doesn't work or feel good. We can live this way for a time, but it will eventually eat away at our insides.

Comfort and wanting God have a core incompatibility. Comfort is incompatible with serving. It is incompatible with radical living. It is incompatible with *God*. So while we may be able to run from service for a time, eventually we won't be able to. The God-call on our life will simply be too loud and too strong. Conversely, when we experience a revival of the soul, finding a cause to get involved in will not be a problem. The response to our want for God will be automatic.

Comfort stops the important conversations, settles us into a complacent life, convinces us we lack good opportunities to serve, justifies our inactivity. It supports spiritual comparison, has us comparing ourselves to people who are doing less than we are, serving less, being less sold out for God, makes us feel better about the things we do not do, and ultimately facilitates pride. It hushes the God moanings inside and tells us, *No need to listen. You love God. That is enough.*

And flesh likes what it hears.

It costs us our self-worth

Comfort and self go hand in hand, because comfort is self's greatest indulgence. It is our pleasure center, the place we go to when we are scared or insecure or feeling spiritually rebellious. And Satan knows this. He knows that if he can keep us comfortable, he can manipulate our flesh. He is not Lord over us (because he can't be when we belong to God), but we have given him a level of access to us by choosing ourselves over God. Because loving God and wanting God more will always mean that He is loved more than ourselves. And that thought makes the evil one tremble because of what it means for the Kingdom.

> Comfort is incompatible with serving. It is incompatible with radical living. It is incompatible with *God.*

I won't forget the first time I heard about missionary Martin Burnham, the man who was killed by a terrorist group in 2002 during a rescue attempt by the Philippine military. He and his wife, Gracia, had been serving the jungle people and telling them about God for 15 years when they were kidnapped and held hostage. In his attempt to flee from his captors he was shot and killed while his wife lay injured. Martin died somewhere between jungle trees, having chosen to serve God to the very last breath of his life.

I'm moved by how much this man must have wanted God in

order to leave the comforts of his life in the States. He lived a life of risk, surely knowing this outcome was possible. I wonder how many times Satan tried to talk him out of it. I wonder how he tried to trip him up, dangling comforts in front of him to make him second-guess his desire and loyalties. I wonder if he whispered manipulative words to Martin…like he does to us when our passion for God burns and we are right on the cusp of doing something radical for Him.

Satan knows of our potential for the Kingdom and he knows of the internal erosion that happens when we choose self over God. While for a time we may be able to justify not doing more for God or experiencing the joy of Kingdom work more fully, we will never (no, never) escape the voice inside that calls us out of the comfort zone and into the glorious unknown of God. It's in there for good. There's no getting rid of it. It can be muffled, ignored, or temporarily forgotten. But it will never go away, no matter how far from it we run. When we don't defy our comfort it leads to a settled-in climate of laziness and apathy, which in turn leads to guilt because we make less of our life. Our potential cries within and it can't completely be silenced. And so, eventually, we wake in the morning with a feeling of inexplicable despair. We ask, *Why, with all I have and all the wonderful things around me, am I not happy?* Because we have cheated ourselves, cut our own lives short by being unwilling to give up comfort.

It costs us vibrancy and fellowship

Has comfort ever gotten you anywhere with God?

If I haven't yet convinced you that comfort is ultimately not the best friend you may think it is, I'm not sure anything I write after this will. So don't take my word for it. Think very honestly about your own life, which no one but God and you fully know. Check what

I am saying against what you know to be true and have experienced for yourself.

Has comfort ever gotten you anywhere with God?

Has comfort kept you from things you sense He wants you to do?

Do you live to your full potential? If not, does your desire for comfort play a part in that?

These are questions we must consider.

While God is a God who comforts us,* He is not a God who honors earthly, selfish comfort in our relationship with Him. In Luke 9:23 Jesus tells the gathered crowd, "If any of you wants to be my follower, you must turn from your selfish ways, take up your cross daily, and follow me."

Take up your cross daily. Sound comfortable?

Rather, in all of God's comforting interactions with those in the Bible, comfort came after suffering. Godly comfort was for those who faced real, tough difficulties in the world. The Father was there through it all and after it all to provide the strong shoulder, hold the hand, wipe the tears, and bring peace. Job, for example, faced horrific difficulties. For a long stretch of time there was no physical comfort to be found in the midst of his deep, dark suffering. There was no comfort to be found in his bed; no comfort to be found in sleep. What Job experienced is what we too experience when hard life things consume us: No physical things can provide the comfort we need.

Only God.

> Nothing, no one, can settle our thrashing but God. Apart from Him, we will thrash and struggle forever.

---

* "I, yes I, am the one who comforts you. So why are you afraid of mere humans, who wither like the grass and disappear?" (Isaiah 51:12).

"All praise to God, the Father of our Lord Jesus Christ. God is our merciful Father and the source of all comfort" (2 Corinthians 1:3).

This is where we are in the world, friends. Nothing, no one, can settle our thrashing but God. Apart from Him, we will thrash and struggle forever.

And in a great irony, when we choose comfort, we give up the opportunity to know *His* comfort. We won't know the full measure of God coming to the brokenhearted.* We won't know of the revival. We won't know of the joy. We will thwart that by reaching our goal of being comfortable but immobilizing ourselves in the process. We will miss the opportunities.

Because "we have plenty of hard times that come from following the Messiah, but no more so than the good times of his healing comfort—we get a full measure of that, too" (2 Corinthians 1:5 MSG).

Revival

The thing that will really change us is something most of us are too comfortable to do. It is something a young preacher named Evan Roberts did during the Welsh Revival…something we all can do.

Pray.

Before you turn a deaf ear, convinced you have heard it all on prayer, let me both challenge and enlighten you: Maybe you've never before thought about prayer in the context of *comfort*.

The preacher man Evan Roberts did not just pray to see God move. He got *uncomfortable* with it. He and God would meet every night, in the middle of the night while others were sleeping, and they would talk. One on one. They were inconvenient prayers. They met at an inconvenient time. They were sleep interrupters, time eaters. Roberts prayed every day from one o'clock to four o'clock in the morning.

---

* "The high and lofty one who lives in eternity, the Holy One, says this: 'I live in the high and holy place with those whose spirits are contrite and humble. I restore the crushed spirit of the humble and revive the courage of those with repentant hearts'" (Isaiah 57:15).

Most of us don't pray like this. We don't get up in the middle of the night to talk to the Father on a regular basis, and if we do, we are blessed to be among the few who have seen the fruit of such prayers and are convinced of the benefits. What would happen in our lives, to our world, if we would be willing to be inconvenienced and pray most of our nights away?

We can complain about the condition of our world and worry ourselves into the night hours about the church, our kids, our problems, but until we pray, nothing will change. Why, then, don't we?

Because prayer requires discomfort. It's why I believe we have to get to the point where we are sickened by what our comfort has cost us. Comfort has cost us prayers in the night for those who are lost while we are lying in our bed watching TV. Comfort has cost us spiritual breakthroughs for our kids while we have spent hours on social media posting pictures of them. Comfort has cost us seeing God work in amazing ways while we text our day away in complaints to friends about why our lives are a wreck.

We talk too much and pray too little. We worry too much and pray too little. We choose sleep. We choose our friends, our family, our vacations, our kid's basketball game schedule. We neglect prayer, and then we lament not feeling close to God.

But oh, friend, do you want the truth? Comfort keeps us from knowing the secret places of God. It's not because He is ambivalent or wants to keep us in suspense or on some crazy scavenger hunt to collect the clues to find Him. No, He's not that God. He's this God:

> I publicly proclaim bold promises. I do not whisper obscurities in some dark corner. I would not have told the people of Israel to seek me if I could not be found. I, the LORD, speak only what is true and declare only what is right (Isaiah 45:19).

But He's also a God who requires action from His children, particularly in the area of prayer. "Ask me and I will tell you remarkable secrets you do not know," says Jeremiah 33:3.

Comfort keeps us from having godly insight, not because He does not want to share with us rich, beautiful things our human minds cannot know, but because of our lack of intention toward the knowing. God wants to let us in on so many things we would otherwise not know. But we don't pursue that. Our comfort won't let us.

But there is good news.

Right now is a great moment to start a new longing.

Let me explain.

Before I do, forgive the big sigh. I'm going to need to talk to you about my weight and food and for me, that's a tough subject.

It's something I've never quite been able to conquer. My entire life has been about eating everything I want to eat when I want to eat it and wishing to still be healthy and thin. It's an impossibility, I know, but it just feels unfair for me to go my whole life not pleasuring myself with food. As my friend Rebecca said when we both turned 40, "I think I'm too old to eat food I don't like anymore." (Amen, Rebecca. AMEN.)

But this issue goes further for me than food. It's really about indulgence and comfort and *self*. I don't like to be told no. I don't want to deprive myself in order to be skinny. I want to be wise with my food intake but not enough to give up the things that taste good in my mouth.

So just recently, after months of waking up to a bloated face in the mirror, standing in my full-to-the-brim closet which holds almost nothing I can wear, lamenting the way I feel most every day, my brain switches to a place it hasn't been in years, maybe ever. I don't just want to lose weight; I want to be healthy.

But it isn't about a diet. I've done those for years. I know every calorie count and fat gram and sugar count and could probably be a registered dietician with all the knowledge I have at this point. I've been on the soup diet and the starvation diet and the pills to help you lose weight diet and the stick your finger down your throat and throw up your food so you don't gain weight diet. I've spent days in seminary studying God while living off only Skittles and Diet Coke. No, it isn't about a diet; it is about *more*. It is about discipline and becoming a different person—someone who doesn't always comfort herself with food. It is, in a very strange way, about a longing for my greater desire—my desire for God.

And when this shift in what I want happens—this decision to hate the comfort that has gotten in my way—I am gloriously surprised to find that I gain something *more*.

Soon after, I am in my car, driving through bright orange construction cones to the only healthy food store within 20 miles of me. On this day I do not really have time, but I am determined. This store has the most delicious nitrate-free sliced turkey breast I have ever eaten. It is satisfying, far more so than the regular turkey I buy at the grocery store, and distance and construction zone or not, it is my mission to get it.

> People who are used by God aren't born more special. They've just tasted something good and kept coming back for it. They live with a different longing.

I am motivated by my taste buds. I have tasted the two-minute-away-grocery-store kind, and it was adequate until I started eating the whole foods store's turkey. And now I am hooked on the better kind, unwilling to settle any longer, willing to drive through construction in an almost hour-long round trip instead of going around the corner because my longing has changed. It didn't change until I tried something new and better.

It is this way with us when it comes to settling for a life of comfort over the radical and exciting life of God. People often say to me, "I want God to use my life, but it seems like He always uses someone else. Why won't He use me?" There are hundreds, thousands, maybe millions of us who feel this way. But we have the wrong idea. We assume things. We mistakenly believe He created some people more usable and special.

But it's not true. People who are used by God aren't born more special. They've just tasted something good and kept coming back for it. They live with a different longing. Some people can be bold and loud and out-front about it. Some stay quiet, in the background. There is no pattern or formula: God can use anyone. If we only knew how amazing a life with God tasted we would stop fighting so hard to stay comfortable and safe. We would loathe anything that tasted any different.

So how do we start this revival for God in the midst of comfort?

We put ourselves in positions that constantly expose us to the transformative work of God.

Then we will know better.

And our tastes will eventually change.

Questions for Reflection

1. What is the trade-off for being comfortable in our lives?

2. How does the principle of the greater desire come into play in regard to comfort?

3. What is the issue of the Band-Aid all about? What two ways does it show up most often?

4. In this chapter we read, "We have to get to the point where we are sickened by what our comfort has cost us." What *has* it cost you?

5. How does comfort cushion us from our own reality? Why is this so damaging?

6. What does it feel like to know that comfort keeps you from the secret places of God? Besides prayer, what is one way you can position yourself to begin wanting God more and comfort less?

7. Do you crave revival in this area of your life? What will that look like for you?

Take Your Own Inventory

1. I think about how I will be affected before I do what God asks me to do. True / False

2. I base at least 50 percent of my decisions on how comfortable something is. True / False

3. I have neglected to do something for God because it felt too costly. True / False

4. I quit using my gift when it stretched me further than I wanted. True / False

5. I have a tendency to serve my immediate needs rather than be willing to be uncomfortable while I wait. True / False

6. I have used people or things as Band-Aids for a period of time in my life. True / False

7. Sometimes I feel like I will always be who I am now and won't ever change. True / False

8. I have sometimes felt guilty or sad because I haven't done the things for God I felt led to do. True / False

9. God is not as vibrant in my life as He could be because I'm too settled in. True / False

10. I want revival in this area of my life and to be freed from being comfort-driven. True / False

3

I Want God
More Than Logic and Reason

God has set Eternity in our heart, and man's infinite capacity cannot be filled or satisfied with the things of time and sense.

F.B. MEYER

Back when we had permed hair and were twenty-something-vibrant, we used to talk about how we hoped God would never send us as missionaries to Africa.

My best friend and I recently revisit this 20-year-old conversation: how while we walked the halls of a seminary where we studied God, we secretly feared a call on our lives that would make us do something radical and hard. Now, on one hand, we cringe at this. We want to judge it and call it ignorance or selfishness or being really young or thinking life was just up to us...but then we step back, pause, and get honest.

Were we really that different from most believers? We say we want God but sit with fingers crossed behind our backs, hoping He will never ask us to do something too radical or hard.

The truth is, our fear was never really about Africa. Africa just represented something that was foreign and messy and sacrificial. Africa got blamed for what was really

Bottom Line

Let God break your rules.

73

a small faith—a mind-set whereby we could love God but never let that love interrupt our plan for a beautiful house, a handsome husband, three kids, a dog or two, manicured nails, church on Sunday, and cute jeans. It was never about Africa. It was about wanting life both ways.

Somewhere in the midst of the daily whirlwind of life, we have convinced ourselves that we can live in the in-between when it comes to God. We are convinced we can make our faith what we want it to be—customize it like we do with food at restaurants, ordering faith to fit our tastes. But when we become followers of Christ, we don't get to make up the script. It's either all God or no God, He says.

I think of the church at Laodicea and feel akin. If I'm honest, I also feel scared and convicted. God is always blunt and to the point. But these verses are awakeners of a different kind.

> I know you inside and out, and find little to my liking.
> You're not cold, you're not hot—far better to be either
> cold or hot! You're stale. You're stagnant. You make me
> want to vomit (Revelation 3:15-16 MSG).

The idea that I could make God want to vomit chills me to the bone.

But I am the church at Laodicea. We are the church at Laodicea. We may be more hot than we are cold, less stale and stagnant than we used to be, and, indeed, we should be grateful for the forward progress. But God doesn't compare us to ourselves as the measuring stick. He compares us to *Him*.

Our desire for logic and reason—that which makes sense to us—is one of the biggest factors in why we don't have more of God. It's not that God is displeased with our logic or that we shouldn't seek spiritual understanding through the studying of Scriptures. In fact, this is the essence of spiritual growth: We want more of God the more we know Him. But if we truly want God, the piece that must be abandoned is our demand for logic. We have to want Him more than what we can understand since intellect gets in the way of unvarnished love. When we demand that God make sense, we overstep our role and show our sense of entitlement. In life, God calls us to scary places we can't understand, and we must have an open heart of faith to take the leap with Him. We must come as children who know and care nothing of formulas, calculations, and risk. That is faith. That makes a Father glad.

Life with God was never meant to be a calculated risk; it was meant to be an illogical surety. Logical people are at risk of stepping in the way of the supernatural. We don't mean to—it's just that often there's a core incompatibility between what is known (tangible, flesh, earth) and the Unknown (God), and when we choose logic it hinders His work. Don't misunderstand—God doesn't need us to understand to do His thing. He can work under any conditions, at any time, in any way. But whether we submit to His working is in our hands.

> God calls us to scary places we can't understand, and we must have an open heart of faith to take the leap with Him.

He wanted us to choose things and see things and experience things from a free will and open heart. Otherwise, He would have created robots to simply do His bidding. But He didn't. Because He is God, a part of Him will always be unknown to us as humans with limited minds. Yet so much of Him can be known by way of Scripture, experience, the heart, the mind, and the senses. We don't need logic and reason to know we love and trust God.

And while logic feels good because it is a controllable entity, God often calls us to the illogical and unreasonable places to expose what position control holds in our life. He calls us to our *Africa*—the things we fear because they're foreign, messy, and require sacrifice. The things we don't want to face because they seem too hard.

I wonder: **What is your Africa?**

It took 25 years, but my best friend finally met hers.

It started with a simple phone call, an inquiry about orphans in her county who needed a home, but it really started before that. The heart change had to come first, and did. It started seven years before with a trip to Colorado for couples struggling in their marriage. She went with her husband, fighting long-held demons. But she came back herself having changed. My best friend wasn't the same best friend when she came back. She was a better version of the same one I loved. Something inside of her had met God in a different way in those Colorado mountains—something that made her more God-hungry than ever before. She was just…*different*.

So I wasn't completely surprised when she called me a few years later to tell me the news. "We're going to look into foster care, Lisa. I don't have a clue what I'm doing. I just feel pulled to do this and I can't explain why."

I didn't need her to explain. I knew from my own life that wanting God means doing things that move His heart—which we want to do. People will no longer have to pitch us on God-causes; our heart for Him compels us to pursue them.

And I knew this, too—that God doesn't typically ready us in ways we think work best and look best to others. He readies us on the inside when we can't see it ourselves. (It's a myth to think we will ever be ready for anything that is a God-sized undertaking. We can position ourselves, but can never fully prepare.) My friend would never be ready to do foster care. But she was already ready to do it because of her desire for Him.

It has now been two years. My best friend and her family are full into their *Africa*. There have been hundreds of phone calls since, maybe a thousand, where she cries in frustration because it's hard. I tell her I love her but offer little more than that because I just can't help like God. There have been children who bite her, spit on her, and keep her awake at night telling her they hear voices. She's qualified for none of it. There have been stains on new carpet and walls coated with dirt and sketchy teenage boys approaching her car because she has a foster son with her who has never had a parent tell him drugs aren't okay. And none of it makes sense.

But it's *God*. It's now what she knows. It's why in spite of the hundreds of hot tears, the moments of despair, and the life that feels at times like it's going off the rails, their family keeps taking orphans in—keeps going.

We have both learned much since those seminary days. About life, God, and what *messy* looks like. We have learned that *Africa* is not always Africa and life is not our script to write and God lives in the illogical sureties, which are abundantly superior to the calculated risks.

And there is much more to learn.

But some things about God, we never will.

So we keep going and make peace with the not knowing, understanding it is an important part of wanting Him first and most.

The Hard Things and the Good Things

Choosing for ourselves is a two-sided gift.

It's maybe His greatest and yet most cruel gift to us: how we get to live a life of choices. Because life is full of dual lovers—both of them pulling, both of them asking, both of them attractive in their own way—and we are often caught in the middle, where even when we choose one we will long for the other. It's the way the flesh rolls, longing for the thing it does not pick.

And yet there comes a time when after we understand that the choice is really between everything else and God and we choose Him, the *everything else* becomes far less appealing. Sometimes that surprises even us.

To other people, we become a novelty. We are not used to seeing people who are singly focused on one lover, especially the One who is known through faith.

What we see and know in everyday life is that people who stand out for God don't always have things as easy. And on a human, core level, this scares us. Because everything in our life since birth has pounded in our head that the highest level of achievement is to be seen, known, and lauded. And living a life of scary *Africas* for God just doesn't fit into that scenario. So for many of us, it takes a complete rewiring.

And I know it's hard to believe that we who are so wired to choose a life that makes sense can ever make peace with the *not knowing* about God; that logic and reason do not have to be the lovers that win; that we will ever be okay with our brains not understanding. But it's true. And I know this not because I have it all conquered and tied up with a pretty bow, but because I believe the Bible. And the Bible tells me that people who did not know what God was doing chose Him and not logic anyway, even at their own expense.

Abraham: went to a foreign place without knowing where he was going.

Rahab: risked her own life to save strangers.

Noah: built a massive boat he didn't need for at least 20 years.

Esther: went before the King, risking being beheaded.

The Bible is full of examples like these. In fact, with every Bible hero runs a thread of the seemingly illogical. These people were brave and unique, but they were human, and not God, which gives me great hope. It tells me that we too have the capacity to choose Him over what seems to make sense on the outside.

I know what you may be thinking. It's hard to choose God over logic and reason when He is silent for a period of time, allows things we love to be taken away, and doesn't deliver on our expectations. *True*. And I think we should know going in that the choice for God will not always come with welcome results. Sometimes it will come with ridicule. Sometimes it will be met with anger. Sometimes it will be accompanied by misunderstanding and (as crazy as it sounds) sometimes it will be greeted by jealousy. Because when we choose the path of God, the one less taken, other people react to their own unwillingness. And sometimes, though it really has nothing to do with us, it seems as if it does.

Ridicule

Think Noah's ark. The Bible doesn't say specifically, but scholars believe it took between 20 and 75 years to build the massive boat that would save Noah, his family, and the animals from the waters God was about to unleash in a flood. And don't we know from human nature that during those many years the people who watched Noah work tirelessly on this big boat had some things to say about it?

"Uh, what exactly are you building, dude?"

"Did God tell you to build that big boat thing? You sure it wasn't a little too much wine one night?"

"Noah, I love you man, but you are looking crazy out here building that thing for no good reason. Why don't you give it up and come hang out with the boys for a while?"

But Noah was not deterred. He didn't cave when he was questioned. He didn't put his tools down and leave them to rust when he encountered pushback. He wasn't swayed by sarcasm or ridicule. Instead, he kept working, building, preparing. He trusted the promise of God without needing more information. And of course God was right. The flood Noah had prepared for came one day, fast and furious.

If we are to want God more than the logic we are accustomed to, we, too, will have to stop needing more information. There will be times when people will see our soul revival and dismiss us as radical. Especially in this day, when truth is often watered down, moral absolutes are not valued, and vocal God-followers are few, those who live in that space are often seen as fanatics. Spiritual zealots. It is not the most popular place to be.

And in those times we will have to learn to let the promise of God, which rings in our ears, drown out the sarcasm and skepticism of the world that says we are crazy for doing things in a way that doesn't make good human sense. We will have to keep working, keep building, keep preparing, with the steadfast belief that He doesn't have to make sense to be Sovereign.

Anger

King Nebuchadnezzar had built a massive golden statue in his likeness and commanded that everyone in the kingdom bow down to it. And everyone did—everyone but Shadrach, Meshach, and Abednego. Daniel 3:19 tells us that "Nebuchadnezzar was so furious with Shadrach, Meshach, and Abednego that his face became distorted with rage." His anger was so strong that he threw the men into a flaming furnace for them to die. If we know the story, we know that not only did they not die, but they stepped out of the fiery room untouched. They didn't even smell like smoke.

And yet all along, no one but God had known how it would all turn out. The three young men just believed. They trusted. But they did not have the mind of God, so they ultimately did not *know*.

Logic would have said, *You will burn for your disobedience to the King.* Reason would have cajoled, *Follow the rules and do what the King says so you can stick around to be an influence for God.* But logic and reason aren't the rules of God. He leads in other ways, God ways, that don't travel in that box. His ways say, *It won't make sense but do it anyway. You don't have to see. You don't have to know. You just have to trust.*

Sometimes, when we choose God over logic and reason, we will make people angry. Our family and friends may be angry because it appears we are getting taken advantage of, making foolish moves, and denying our God-given ability to use our brains. People on the outside looking in may become convicted by their own comfort-zone living but deflect their inner turmoil by making us the object of their anger, accusing us of being high-and-mighty out-of-touch judgmental hypocrites. But when something is of God, it does not have to make sense to everyone else. That is why it's vital that before we make bold moves for God we are sure those instructions are truly coming from Him. And how do we know that?

We pray. A lot. *First.*

Misunderstanding

In the book of Acts we read the story of the life of Stephen. Chapter 7 holds the big, beautiful, hard story of his life and death. In a nutshell, Stephen preached things that made the Jewish leaders mad. So they stoned him, and he died.

Preaching at the expense of your life. We know, in our good Christian minds, that it's something we need to be willing to do—that becoming a follower of Jesus Christ means that there may be sacrifice. But most of us have not had this put to the test, at least not in this way.

When we choose God over logic and reason, we will likely be misunderstood. Surely some of the people who witnessed this act against Stephen thought to themselves, *Well, since that ending wasn't good, God couldn't have been in it.* Because sometimes, things end badly. We have been conditioned to think that happy endings are for good people and sad endings are for those who have done something wrong. It goes against everything we know from the Bible about living in a John 16:33* world, of course, but still, we have it in our minds. We

---

* "Here on earth you will have many trials and sorrows. But take heart, because I have overcome the world."

may acknowledge that the world is a troublesome place, but when we encounter it for ourselves the first question we ask is *why*. We misunderstand worldly struggles because we're viewing them from the wrong perspective.

Friends, we do not gain or lose in the world's terms based on our goodness. We live in a troubled place and we let God guide us through it…or we don't.

We might not get the happy ending, which is an important thing for us to know. We'll experience pain and sadness in this world. We'll taste the sting of death. And when we do, logic and reason will never be able to make things okay. Logic and reason will never comfort grieving parents. It will not comfort those desperate for work or those appalled at the injustice they see in the world. It just won't and it can't, because life is not a formula. So God asks us to live without that expectation.

My best friend, the foster mom I told you about, didn't know about the backlash she would encounter when she started taking in kids. She didn't know that church people would not be able to wrap their minds around what she and her family were doing and would react to it in such a strange way. Some of them would no longer look her in the eye. Others would flash a nervous smile as they quickly walked by her in the hall, halfheartedly saying over their shoulder, "Let me know if I can do anything for you!" And then there were the well-meaning ones, more than she could count, who would say that one thing that would sting the most: "I don't think I could ever give up kids. I'm just not wired that way."

As if she was. As if this woman who was also a mother had some kind of amazing love-them-and-leave-them wiring that made her qualified to take kids in, give them a home for months on end, feed them, help them brush their teeth, diaper their bottoms, wipe their tears, hear their hurts, and then heartlessly send them on their way.

As if anyone who lives their *Africa* has the ability to do it in and of themselves.

It's not that the good church people wanted to be hurtful or callous. It's just that they misunderstood. They mistook *servant of God* for *qualified employee*. They thought *résumé* instead of *surrender*. In that deep-down place, they wanted to find a reason why someone could do something so messy and raw and hard and they couldn't. Because if they could say they *couldn't* then they wouldn't have to say they just weren't *willing to*.

Friends, I'd like to paint a prettier picture. I'd like to lie and say that if we want God more and pursue God more than logic and reason we will have more friends and be completely understood. But it's not true. And if, like me, you fear being misunderstood almost more than you fear anything else, surrender can feel scary. We will never be qualified to do anything God-sized; all we can ever be is willing.

Sometimes we will question what God puts in our hearts. We will think we have lost our own mind. We will shake in our boots the same way anyone else would. We will have moments of panic and pain and fear.

And somehow God will be bigger. I don't know how. He just will.

Jealousy

I ask the question, "Has there been a time you were serving God that you believed/knew someone was jealous of you in that endeavor?" because I am curious how the Facebook world might respond. Within three minutes I get a flood of private messages from friends I barely know and ones I know well, both men and women, all with their stories. "I was chosen to be on a church committee and as a result received such negativity, it literally drove me away from that church and from ever serving again." "When my husband and I began doing ministry, my closest friend distanced herself from me and started acting hateful and nasty." "I knew I was supposed to leave my job and take my family out of the States to go to the foreign mission field, but I still have people who will not talk to me years later because I did and they say they don't agree. I had a good friend tell me that because of my decision he has to hear his wife talk about it all the time and it has made him resent me because he thinks she doesn't respect him the same way she does me. He's admitted to me he is jealous—jealous I am serving God in a way he isn't…jealous I am willing to be radical when he can't shake the desire to stay well-off and safe."

These friends are not alone. Many people who have defied human logic and reason for the greater desire to passionately serve God have been met with opposition. They have had to contend with jealous people who wish their commitment were not so loud and bright. It is hard to be supportive of people who convict us in our complacency, call us out by their life. God-wanters stand in stark contrast to those of us who still want other things more, and it's easy to become jealous of their commitment and passion.

As the late Scottish preacher Alexander Whyte once said, "Those who are deaf always despise those who dance." When people have rules for God—logical and reasonable rules that are calculated and formulated and make good sense—they will not walk in the same freedom. And then will come the jealousy.

We are a people who spend our lives longing to be free—from the past, from insecurity, from pressure and fear and anger and *whatever*. And when we see someone who has that freedom and we don't, we resent them. We are jealous of their passion, jealous of their joy. We are jealous of their contentment and yes, even, their super crazy and unpredictable life. We want what they have, though we are not willing to completely pursue it. So we then become the people who want life both ways.

People will be jealous when you choose God over logic and reason.

They may mask it in a laugh or with probing questions or with statements like, "I could never give up a child. I am just not wired that way." But what they really want is a life like yours. What they really long for is to be able to be free enough to leap and dance, even as they are on this unpredictable journey with God at the wheel. They really want to experience Him being bigger—even when that desire doesn't make sense. They really want the God adventure.

> You will find beauty if you go with God.

We all do.

But please know this: Even in tough moments, you will find beauty if you go with God.

Provision

> Look at the birds. They don't plant or harvest or store food in barns, for your heavenly Father feeds them. And aren't you far more valuable to him than they are? (Matthew 6:26).

Yeah, it was probably tough on Noah while he was building that ark. It couldn't have been easy with all the whispers and laughs and rumors going around. But you know what God gave Noah?

Provision.

He provided for him and his family and even his beloved animals. He gave them a place where they would be safe and dry during the 40-day flood that wiped everyone else out. It wasn't logical for Noah to build that big boat. It didn't make sense as he waited numerous years for the rain to come.

But God always had a plan. He always does. And if, when choosing Him over logic, He asks us to do something that seems hard? He will provide everything we need (but not everything we think we need) to see it through.

In our everyday life, we assume provision to look like something physical—food on our table in generous portions, a roof over our head that won't leak, other physical comforts. But our minds think too small. God's provision goes beyond these things. It is as slave-trader-turned-preacher John Newton (author of the song "Amazing Grace") once said: "God often takes a course for accomplishing His purposes directly contrary to what our narrow views would prescribe. He brings a death upon our feelings, wishes, and prospects when He is about to give us the desire of our hearts."

The desire of our hearts is most often that our physical needs are taken care of, which is a legitimate want. But we are often so focused on getting those needs met that we miss some of the greater things God provides. He provides us with grace when we don't deserve it. He provides us with strength when ours is gone. He provides us with hope when there appears to be no good reason. He provides us with love, joy, and a chance to live another day when we have messed up many of the days He's given us before. These are the things God provides like none other. Wanting God more than logic and reason helps us recognize the true provisions of God.

Protection

> For he will order his angels to protect you wherever you go (Psalm 91:11).

On the outside looking in, Daniel lived the life of a renegade. He refused the food he was mandated to eat and lived on his own diet of vegetables. He told the king hard truths through the interpretation of his dreams. He prayed to his God three times a day even though it violated the law. But though he lived this way, his life was not driven by rebellion or managed in his own hands. God knew every second that what looked to be hopeless situations were all part of the master plan. God knew Daniel would not lose his life until He was ready to take it one day. Daniel believed that too, which was why he was willing to make the bold God-moves that others would only see as colossal risks. He did not need to ask God if he would, in fact, be strong by following the less fatty, indulgent diet. He didn't need to wonder if he should tell the king the truth even though it was going to make him mad. He didn't question God about those lions—whether they would be tranquilized or all their deadly teeth would suddenly fall out (which are all questions I would likely ask). In all of these tough spots, Daniel trusted God would be with him, and He was. He always is. And if He asks us to trust Him in a way that doesn't make sense at the outset, He will provide a covering of protection in ways we may never see.

Sometimes we can see the hand of God protecting us, but many times we cannot. We see the times we narrowly miss that car on the highway running into us, the plane we were supposed to be on that crashed, the relationship we so desperately wanted that didn't work out (and now we see how damaging it would have been if it had). But for everything we see, there is much we do not. God is our full-time protector. In our sleep, when there is nothing we can do for ourselves, He keeps watch. His daily plan always includes being the overseer of our protection. Wanting God over logic and reason comes with an underlying trust on our part and a thorough follow-through on His.

Intimacy

> I will live in them and walk among them. I will be their
> God, and they will be my people (2 Corinthians 6:16).

I'm mesmerized by the whole story of Stephen, but by one detail in particular:

> At that point they went wild, a rioting mob of catcalls and whistles and invective. But Stephen, full of the Holy Spirit, hardly noticed—he only had eyes for God, whom he saw in all his glory with Jesus standing at his side. He said, "Oh! I see heaven wide open and the Son of Man standing at God's side!" (Acts 7:55 MSG).

Stephen only had eyes for God. In the midst of pain, misunderstanding, rejection, and yes, even death, Stephen only had eyes for God. That a man could be in those conditions and gaze with loving eyes on the Almighty, who keeps the world spinning on its axis and has command over everything…yet doesn't save His own child from horrible, cruel death? A logical impossibility. But this is the irony about a relationship with God. We aren't promised death will not come. In truth, we are promised it will. Hebrews 9:27 reminds us that "each person is destined to die." We are told life will be full of heartache.

But in the midst of that heartache, we walk with an unseen God who meets needs that go beyond the merely physical. Where a hug can ease a sorrow and a friend can soothe, God will come closer. His scent will linger long after the embrace ends. Stephen was dying, but even in that death came intimacy. God brings intimacy to the heart that chooses Him.

In the great fractures of our lives, God is present in the cracks.

I think of my college friend who recently lost her husband, my church friend who recently lost her son, my cyber friend who is fighting cancer. All of them have testified with their own lips about the intimacy of God in these hell-on-earth scenarios where otherwise, no alleviation of pain could come. They have all spoken of the sustaining hand of God to pick them up from the cold, black ditch they have landed in—and how that's the only way they would ever get out. They speak with wet eyes of Him holding their broken universe together, though their hearts still hurt. And in the great fracture of their life, God is present in the cracks. This, my friend, is intimacy.

Endorsement

I have called you by name; you are mine (Isaiah 43:1).

Nothing feels worse than rejection. When someone rejects us, our insides wither and cry and sometimes harden and threaten to die. We feel discarded and judged and want to scream at them that we are worthy, and they are wrong for not seeing it. Or we begin to hear lies in our head that whisper *maybe they are right,* which take us down a road of self-loathing we often waste years trying to find our way off of. Jealousy leads people to reject us. But then, *God.*

This is the gift of God: Even in the sting of rejection from others, He strengthens our significance. His voice is louder. He is able, with one heart-to-heart endorsement, to silence the noise of human haters. He does not choose favorites, does not pick teams, does not sway to the pressure of the world's hierarchy of class and race and people. He is simply and beautifully above all that. When we want Him, we gain the greater thing: His endorsement. To be backed by God is the ultimate in life—the ultimate support, the ultimate approval of the person we are. There is nothing we could have that is greater.

Provision. Protection. Intimacy. Endorsement. They will not always come in the way we think and in the moment we think them. My husband will often say, "You can tell me what to do or how to do it, but not both." This, of course, is said tongue in cheek when my female tendency to try to control comes out in such a way he needs to send me a message to back off a bit. But it's a good reminder to me of how I often treat God. I try to tell Him what to do and how to do it and if He could also follow this calendar and time frame I have in mind that would be so appreciated. We want God to make good on His promises and He will, but since His mind is above ours, we may have two very different ideas of what that looks like. And always, in these great gifts and promises, the delivery method is up to Him.

Before we move on, may I say one more thing?

God expects us to be responsible.

So please do not hear this chapter saying we do not need to be wise, weigh consequences, or use our minds when it comes to the things of God. I am not proposing we lose our minds when we come to God. It is biblical to be a person of wisdom and care when it comes to making decisions—even daily ones. Proverbs 3:21 reminds us not to "lose sight of common sense and discernment."

And more than that, God wants us to become students of Him. He asks this of us because He knows that the more we learn about Him, the more we will be drawn to Him and want to know Him more. This is the way He intended, this craving after we've had a taste—that we would search Scripture for ourselves and let the Holy Spirit be our best teacher, with the ultimate goal of knowing God. He assures us in Proverbs 8:17, "Those who search will surely find me," and I've found no better way to search for God than to open up His Word.

Studying theology is not wrong and has in fact helped its students come to know God deeper. In many ways, we have a responsibility to dive deeper into the context of Scripture so the truth will come alive and we won't add our skewed interpretation. There is something wonderful about knowing the *why* behind the life of God and Scripture and at the same time, having the childlike faith to accept that which we may never fully know. A lover of God can live in the space of both.

Wanting God more than logic and reason doesn't mean logic isn't good. It doesn't mean we don't think before we act. It means we don't reason away the things we know in our heart God is drawing us to, even when they don't make logical sense to us or others.

It means not trying to reason away the supernatural.

It means staying open to God breaking the rules, wrecking what we know so He can rebuild our life on faith.

Revival

Nothing about the Welsh Revival made sense. Not the time, not the place, not the people. They were too young, too naïve. Most of the major players were new Christians. Wales was wild and wicked. The longstanding traditions of sin had been well established.

And yet God moved.

This gives us hope for today, takes away our excuses. When we begin to believe God is no longer working and He no longer has His hand on the church, we can remember that the world, since the fall, has always been married to wickedness. (If God's hand was really off us, we would not last a day.)

God does not bring revival based on how good we are. He brings revival to the heart that fully seeks Him. Sometimes that revival becomes corporate.

Though the Welsh Revival took place in 1904-1905, as with every movement of God, the rumblings had begun long before. In the late 1800s, a Welsh pastor leading a successful, thriving church in Scranton, Pennsylvania, began to become aware that his flesh had overtaken his preaching and leading. He began to notice how his passion for God had turned into desire to perform. This grieved him to the point where he decided to resign, return to his beloved homeland of Wales, and urge his countrymen to seek revival.

It is always the revival of the heart, first, that sparks great movements of God. What God was doing in this pastor's heart was preparation for what He would do on a greater scale in the years to come.

After being maligned and criticized and ridiculed, this Welsh pastor with a heart burning for God began to see God move. The heart of revival started in him. But now, revival was making its way into the hearts of others.

This is what happens, friends: A heart of revival will always affect others. It is why we read blogs from servants who go on mission trips and suddenly, our hearts are pulled to serve. We hear stories of God's work through normal, everyday people in the inner city, rescues of girls from sex trafficking, a boy running into a burning building to save an elderly woman in her helplessness, and in this place we are moved by the human impossibility of it all and the hope that we can, too.

This is God.

Revival comes with a surrendering of logic. It is holding open the hands and laying down the need for reason. It is a deference to the heart and mind of God and the willingness to receive even that from Him which does not make sense. It is grasping onto the illogical sureties that God will provide even in the desert. That He will be enough in moments that nothing else is. We will never see God in the way we want if we hold on to a solo reliance upon our logic. Revelation doesn't come to closed hearts and minds.

When Evan Roberts, the young man who would eventually become the Welsh Revival's most popular evangelist, went to preach in all the places God led him, he could not take his logic with him or he would have left the side of God. He knew, as we must know, that leaving God's side in the midst of a work He is doing is the surest way to cut off the work, and Roberts would not do it. So he would go and preach in the places where he was sent, logical or not. And sometimes, if the Spirit of God told him not to preach but just to pray, even when the congregation came with the expectation of hearing, he would sit silently and never take the stage. It didn't have to make sense to Evan. It just had to be entrusted to God.

> Revelation doesn't come to closed hearts and minds.

There is one thing I can promise you: Your flesh will continue to argue this point, want what it wants, makes pitches for the known vs. the unknown.

Because we understand ponies. We understand ice cream and life jackets and swimming. We understand picture frames and air-conditioning and ovens that cook food. But we don't understand life. We don't understand God. On this earth, we never will, and sometimes that frustrates.

And in those moments of non-understanding we will want to take matters into our own hands and build a bubble. We will want to build a bubble that will hold our entire family and everything we love in it—our house, our cars, our church, our future. And we will even be willing to fly on planes to foreign countries for short mission trips in that bubble and do benevolent human things like stand out in the cold and ring bells to collect money in red buckets. In that bubble we will take meals to people in need and talk to our children about God. We will visit the elderly in nursing homes. As long as we're doing good in our bubble, we're okay.

But it's not okay with God. So there will come a point where the bubble can't be included in the picture—where we say yes to God without the safety net, outside of the bubble we've built. And that will take faith—faith in the things we will never understand, the things we aren't supposed to understand but want to, anyway. Faith that we will be okay without the bubble.

Oh, that we would entrust it all to God. All the details of our lives—the daily *it* that consumes us. What places could God move us? What places could He send us to do His work? What places could we find that hold riches we, in our logical life, cannot know? We don't know because we don't trust. And somehow we have believed this idea that it's riskier to follow God than it is to follow what we know. It's a lie, friends. Risk is never on the God side of things.

Year after year, the logical bones rattle and creak and cry out for the moment to be brave and defy what they know. As John Wayne is supposed to have said, "Courage is being scared to death and saddling up anyway."

Today is a good day to saddle up since conditions never have to be perfect for God to do something great. It's a myth that we must wait to have it all figured out before we can move forward with God. God doesn't want us to have the future mapped out. He just wants us to be okay with not knowing all the information before we become heart-willing to move. He is looking for people who will surrender their logic, move when they are scared, and pray like crazy that He will bring revival to their hearts, first, and then to the hearts of others.

And so, right now, this prayer.

> *God, that our bones would creak for You. That we would stop trying to be so smart, stop trying to understand, stop trying to make You make sense. Forgive us; this is what we know. Help us be okay with the not knowing and saddle up anyway. Bring revival to the logical bones and let us step boldly wherever You call. Amen.*

Questions for Reflection

1. What does it mean to you to want life both ways?

2. Have you ever had an *Africa* in your life—something that seemed too messy or risky or hard? How did you respond to it?

3. "Life with God was never meant to be a calculated risk; it was meant to be an illogical surety." Do you agree? What is an illogical surety?

4. Have you ever thought about logic as being a control factor in your life? How does this manifest itself and why is this damaging?

5. What is the difference between positioning yourself for a God-sized undertaking and fully preparing yourself for it?

6. Which of the "hard things" (ridicule, anger, misunderstanding, jealousy) of giving up logic for God is hardest for you? Which of the "good things" you conversely gain (provision, protection, intimacy, endorsement) is the most appealing?

7. Do you crave revival in this area of your life? What will that look like for you?

Take Your Own Inventory

1. It's very important to me that things make sense.
   True / False

2. I have a tendency to live in the great in-between—
   wanting God but also wanting life as I know it.
   True / False

3. I base at least 50 percent of the way I respond to
   something God asks me on calculated risk. True / False

4. I get frustrated with God when I can't figure Him out or
   He doesn't make sense. True / False

5. My intellect keeps me from a childlike faith in God.
   True / False

6. Control holds a significant position in my life.
   True / False

7. I am more eager to do something for God if it seems to be
   a good idea. True / False

8. I am convinced I can properly prepare myself for a
   God-sized undertaking. True / False

9. I fear being ridiculed, misunderstood, or judged for doing
   something that God wants me to do but seems to be
   radical. True / False

10. I want revival in this area of my life and to be freed from
    being logic-driven. True / False

I Want God
More Than Popularity

*There's trouble ahead when you live only for the approval
of others... Your task is to be true, not popular.*

Luke 6:26 msg

In the months before I write this book, I go to a concert with
my daughter. It's one of those concerts where good seats cost as
much as mortgage payments and lots of squealing young girls show
up in glitter.

After driving for hours, we park what seems like 4,000 miles away
from the building and begin walking toward the giggles, conversations,
and screams. "Maybe we should have made a sign," my girl says as
we move closer toward the madness, which I immediately determine
to mean *lame mom for not suggesting it*. But my girl is not sad. She is
far too excited for that. The long-awaited day has arrived, and we are
nearly in *his* presence.

In the chilly night air, we fall in line and wait.
After a few minutes' waiting, my introvert kicks
in, begging me to escape the madness of estrogen that is surrounding me and my girl. I
clutch her closer as the sea of females now
begins to move like minnows heading
downstream toward the open doors, though

Bottom Line

People can't be your
god. God is.

97

she is too caught up to notice we are small and outnumbered and moving involuntarily.

Tickets in hand, we find our seat without incident (the manic mom with purple hair extensions cutting in front of us notwithstanding). Surveying our spot we smile, hug, and settle in. *Kudos to you, Lisa, I think to myself. You have pulled this off and made your girl happy!* My heart is full, which as all parents know, is what happens when our child is content and somehow we haven't managed to mess that up.

The music starts, as loud as you can imagine, and soon *he* arrives, in wings. It is an entrance fit for a kid who has singlehandedly secured the attention of millions of females by way of Instagram selfies of his abs and hair. The confetti blows. The crowd goes wild. My daughter turns to me in tears, asking me to fish a piece of confetti out of her eye.

I do, with one eye still on the wings. There's screaming—lots of screaming—and suddenly I feel like I'm 12 again. I want to dance and put posters up in my room and backwards skate in legwarmers. It is only when the confetti has been fished out and the preteen girls sitting next to me begin to shout loudly, "Father my children!" that I enter back into the moment. And I become 41 again and want to cover my daughter's ears from such things that suggest to her this might even be an option.

We are halfway through the concert when *he* comes to the end of the stage, a runway cross of sorts, and stops and stands. At this point, the shirt has been forsaken. The pants are still on, leather and black, but are so low I find myself praying, *Please help his hip bones be at least big enough to hold the things on.* I do not want *that* kind of show.

He holds an Abercrombie and Fitch model pose and stares for what seems like hours, gazing into the center section of the sea of female, listening to the collective scream. Then, with great fanfare, the head turns to the left, to the estrogen over there. Same model pose. Same pants almost falling down. Same stare. Same collective scream.

This happens at least three more times, until every part of the arena is covered and 30,000 girls are convinced *he's* looked at *her*.

The massive screens behind *him* light up, flashing videos of a little boy long (but not really that long) ago. *He* is singing and playing drums that are really seat bottoms of kitchen chairs with bare hands and it is all so cute none of us in the audience can stand it. We are all reminded that the star, this young icon who holds the attention of the world, was once young and innocent and just a little boy who loved the music.

I do not judge him, but I cannot help but see how popularity has changed *him*. Because it used to just be about the music. And now he's too popular for that. And in the midst of pumping songs and pre-teen girls shouting I wonder, *Does he ever wish it were still just about the music?* If nothing else, life had to have been more simple.

Popularity never lets life be about simple things because it serves a bigger agenda. It changes the core of what we want and dictates what we feel we must do. It takes away our ability to live without an angle. Instead, we serve the god of people so they will stay happy, like this performer now has to do.

And what are we really talking about here, since most of us live in a world that does not include being on a stage with thousands of screaming fans chanting our name? *Approval.* Our need for people to know us, accept us, favor us over others. It is an innate need inside of us—we are no different from the performer in many ways. We too want people to love us. We too crave the idea of importance and being known. We too, in our everyday jeans and everyday hair and every-day jobs, desire to feel big, not small. We don't want to be one of many. We want to be *someone.*

We think of the *performers*—the singers, the actors, the TV stars, and yes, even the ministry leaders—as needing to be popular, not our-selves. But at the core, isn't that really what all of our striving is? Doesn't it feed our incessant need to be admired, well-liked, appealing, *popular*? That, my friend, is universal.

We want approval. We need approval.

We want to be loved. We want friends, and we want people to like us.

And this in itself is not bad. Friends are good. Being liked and loved is good. But the lengths we go to get it from other people put us in a dangerous position of compromise.

We'll never change who we are, we say. We mean it until someone comes along and asks us to be different and, out of fear of not having their approval, we change.

We'll never water down our convictions. We mean this too, until something we hold dear is tested and we are more afraid of being misunderstood or rejected than we are loyal to a standard for our life.

We'll never let people dictate how we do things and what things we will do. But we do. All the time. The things we say *yes* to when we really need to say *no*. The times we have gone places we don't need to go and said things we shouldn't have said and acted ways we shouldn't have acted because we were trying to please other people. And strangely, gradually, in all these scenarios we find ourselves giving people what they want rather than being who we are.

I talk to my friend Wendy about this over lunch at my house. She has come to hang out with me over sandwiches, which is one of our favorite friend things to do. Wendy is not famous. She has no Twitter account, has no ambition to ever write a book or sing songs from a stage. Her daily life consists of family, God, and home—cleaning, running concessions at her son's ball games, taking her grandmother to Panera, feeding her dog. She is a beloved and cherished daughter and wife and mother and friend, and that is her beautiful reality. She is content in her life and one of the most secure people I have ever known. Wendy doesn't see herself as having a desire to be popular since she is one of the rare few I've ever met who is able to go through life without caring much what other people think. So when I mention it, she at first resists this idea that wanting popularity might even be a problem, and I'm skeptical myself.

But as we talk about what popularity in the everyday really looks like—doing things to gain approval, wanting people to like and accept her, having said *yes* to things when she wanted to say *no*—she considers it. "Yes, maybe that is me wanting to be popular." She tilts her head to the left, pensively, and says, "I just don't think of myself that way since I'm not trying to be famous."

We may not be trying to be famous, but we, the everyday people, still want to be popular. We still want attention and kudos and accolades. We still want significance and for people to know our names. That all seems harmless, but those desires so easily slide into an unhealthy place where we ask people to give us things to make us feel worthy. And it gets in the way of wanting God, because other people's attention suddenly takes center stage instead of Him. When we give ourselves away to other people, we can never fully give our whole selves to God.

God didn't create people to become other people's gods. He knows that when we become other people's gods we will not fight the same, love the same, risk the same. He knows we won't preach the same. He knows we will settle more and become watered-down people. He knows we will have to consider our image above everything else and that will extinguish passion flames and truth-telling and free speech. He knows it will make us dilute bitter-tasting truth so people can swallow it better.

> God didn't create people to become other people's gods.

And oh, we are resourceful and smart. We are but one YouTube video away from being famous and known and popular, even if it is for doing basically nothing. We have watched some achieve this instant gratification, which shortcuts having to invest in real relationships, be who we say we are, and exist in a place where we are not known by masses of people. In this starving-for-attention culture, the everyday and ordinary do not feel like enough.

My teenage son tells me the other day his friend wants to be Vine famous. I ask him, "For what?" and he laughs as he says, "Mom, for nothing, really. It's just being Vine famous." I know this is true because I hear my kids talk about their peers on Vine, the video making app, who have two million followers who basically just watch them brush their teeth and talk about things that annoy them. It's proof that we want attention, or we think we do. Our standards are so low that we almost don't care by what means we gain that recognition. We just want to lay our heads down at night feeling like we matter. We live in a culture that says *make me popular* while Jesus says *become less*. **It's a daily fight to want God more than ourselves when our worlds are at odds.**

In John 12, during the height of Jesus's healing and miracles, even after the whole raising Lazarus from the dead thing, we learn that "most of the people still did not believe in him" (John 12:37). Jesus was a polarizer, not what we typically aim for when we dream of being popular, though it is the reality of anyone who lives big and bold: loved by some, hated by others. And He was most bothered by those who believed yet didn't speak up. Other people, many people, including some of the Jewish believers, *did* believe. They believed He was Who He said He was and would do what He claimed to do and had, in fact, come to save the world. But they stayed silent in their belief.

> We will only want Him more, only live for Him more, when our need to get attention and approval stops being a part of the equation.

> Many people did believe in him, however, including some
> of the Jewish leaders. But they wouldn't admit it for fear
> that the Pharisees would expel them from the synagogue.
> For they loved human praise more than the praise of God
> (John 12:42-43).

God doesn't give passes to people who long to be popular and are willing to forgo their first allegiance to Him in the process. He loathes this. Can't and won't turn a blind eye. I know this is not a popular message. But it is *the truth about how popularity works when it comes to God.* We will only want Him more, only live for Him more, when our need to get attention and approval stops being a part of the equation.

It's Him or Us

Let's talk about Jeremiah.

First, you should know going in: I am a fan. Anyone who writes two books of the Bible, preaches to five kings, leads at least one spiritual reformation, has his life threatened on many occasions but still keeps preaching, loves people so much he earns the title of "weeping prophet," and is basically just flat-out nuts about God is fan-worthy, in my book.

But Jeremiah is amazing to me mostly for his belief about popularity, which was basically this: *I don't care what anyone thinks. I am just about God.* Oh, if we emulated this philosophy. If only we had more people who didn't care about the opinions of others. If only we had more people who were just about God. Do you believe as I do, friend, that this world would look different?

Jeremiah preached his guts out, mostly unpopular messages, and never saw people change. Never. As in never, ever, it didn't happen. People didn't put him on billboards or buy tickets to his events and he never sold a bestselling book. But there is no record anywhere of him quitting. Instead, we read about a pounding and perseverance, Jeremiah doing the harder but better thing, cheering other people on, and yes, struggling, but never so much he folds. And as a result, the words he wrote and the life he lived ignite a fire to change under the feet of all of us—we who just wish to be noticed and want to serve God but on our terms and *if it's at all possible, God, please let that include me becoming popular or famous*. If it doesn't, it should.

My friends, it's either Him or us. We don't get it both ways. In the everyday, God may use us to further His message to those around us through coffee shop interactions, neighborhood gatherings, and friends who are our captive and listening audience, waiting to decide if they want God based on how we act, react, and generally manage life. And God may use us on some kind of stage or in some kind of spotlight where there are listeners and watchers so His message gets out there and people move toward Him. *But neither of those scenarios will be anything of us.* When God is gracious enough to use us in either place, we would be better off to never leave our homes than let any of it enslave us to human opinion. **God's message is His. We are narcissists when we make it about us.**

This was Jeremiah's message. It was his life. He didn't have time to waste chasing people down, asking them to believe in him, saying that God was really giving him an amazing message and people should like him because of it. All he had time to do was preach that God was serious and things were in bad shape. He preached beautiful, hard-fought truths like, "If you look for me wholeheartedly, you will find me" (Jeremiah 29:13). He delivered promises for right hearts and right living like, "'I will be found by you,' says the Lord. 'I will end your captivity and restore your fortunes. I will gather you out of the nations where I sent you and bring you home again to your own land" (Jeremiah 29:14). And he relayed gorgeous, breathtaking, undeserving things like, "You will be my people, and I will be your God" (Jeremiah 30:22).

If Jeremiah had chased people down to get them to like his message he wouldn't have been able to preach such things. He would have been too distracted by the god of popularity, which may have made him more liked but could never make him more effective. He would have had to water down truth. After all, popularity causes us to give a skewed version of truth—the version that jockeys for a position of likability.

And the bottom line? God can't use someone who thinks about themselves too much. His eye will rest on the one who is first and foremost about Him. We are all created usable but not everyone gets used. Our desire to be popular with other people hinders God's movement in us. He is a God of free will, and if we choose ourselves over Him, He lets us have our way.

Why We Choose Popularity

Why do we choose popularity over God? It's quite simple: We don't trust Him to be the better choice. And we can argue that until the cows come home, say it isn't so because it sounds so ugly, but why else would we crave the praise of people? If He were enough (like we claim Him to be) would not everything else be a lesser find? Remember John 12:43? "They loved human praise more than the praise of God." The verse is speaking about those in Jesus's day who loved validation from others more than validation from God. We too want this—and we prove it by the way we live our lives.

God doesn't want mere words. He's heard them all, knew them all before our lips even moved to say *Oh God, I love You* and *Oh God, I'll serve You* and *Oh God, use my life* while we kept an eye on those around us, hoping they'd find us worthy. We must lose the taste in our mouth for being known by anyone but God. When popularity is no longer our god, the real God will finally be able to use us.

But until we reach that vital point, we will continue to drown within the rivers of our feelings of unworthiness, ever afraid that we will leave this life without having made anyone's list. Do we not understand that this is an albatross around our necks that keeps us at the bottom? God is waiting on us to choose Him, only Him, always Him, forever Him…and He will release us from every self-inflicted chain that has kept us bound so we can live *free*. But until we allow Him to do what only He can, the elevation of and acceptance by man will continue to keep us bound.

Being afraid

Revisit John 12 with me. Remember why the Word says that people, even some in leadership, didn't want to admit to anyone that they believed in Jesus? It was because of their "fear that the Pharisees would expel them from the synagogue" (John 12:42).

The synagogue was their livelihood. It was the place where they were known. They had carved out a niche and didn't want to lose that status anytime soon. They feared rejection and ridicule. They couldn't bear the thought of losing popularity. And what they say to God in the process of all this is, *I would stand up for You, but You're not worth it.*

We say this to God too. In our everyday life, fear is sneaky. It doesn't always look like we expect. We expect it to be snarly and frothing and hunched over and one-eyed. We don't expect it to look like a conversation with a family member who is questioning our faith over a restaurant appetizer of fried pickles on a Friday night. We want people to love us. We want them to like us. We fear they won't. Our desire to be popular among even our own people has been the cause of many stifled conversations. Subsequently, family members we love are dying and going to hell. This is a stark reality, friends. Choosing popularity over Christ is a high stake that isn't worth the risk.

Our mistake is in thinking we can have it both ways—that we can somehow preserve our reputation and control our PR and simultaneously be a thriving force in the Kingdom. We can't. Whichever we choose, one will lose.

Fear makes people wear masks and rob banks for quick money. It makes women emotionally slice each other with mean words. It keeps believers from joining hands and hearts and praying in unison in a way that Jesus says strengthens the body and moves the heavens. It steals years from men who don't remember the days flying away. It causes good people to keep quiet when they should stand up and robs believers of an amazing God-journey on the other side of trying to be popular.

But God-courage doesn't just come. It doesn't just casually slide into our life while we are busy chasing other things. It comes by one choice today to be brave. And then another brave choice tomorrow. And then, the next time the hard choice comes around, we find we have the courage to make it. But we have to choose that first time. We have to choose God first and then ask Him to help us live that out. And then, before we know it, we have taken the option of being popular off the table and we no longer miss it.

Being ashamed

In hindsight, I see now how my younger life was made up of a series of detriments to my popularity I was trying to avoid. Buckle in for the ride, my friends. It's about to get wildly personal.

I start with the end of the story, only because you should probably know the *what* before the *why*.

Somewhere between the carpool line and burning dinner, I find myself as a grown woman sitting in a tattoo shop with Metallica playing in the background, a shirtless man about to have his shoulder become one with a dragon, and a sleeved-out boy barely older than my son ready to ink me. "Hi, my name is Ryan," he says to me as he and his black chucks amble over. It is clearly not his first rodeo, though his nonchalance doesn't ease me. Everything within me wants to ask him if his mother knows he's doing this or if he is even of voting age, since I am entrusting him to carve into my wrist. But I refrain. The way he's eyeing me, I know he thinks I don't belong in this place, and I'm afraid he's going to say it out loud and send me away. And that makes me panic, since I've decided to do this.

I'm getting a tattoo. It's not my first. But it will likely be my last.

(I must pause here and say that I realize there is nothing special or interesting to people at this point about a tattoo, since many people have them—even soccer moms like me. But it is wildly significant to me because of what it has to do with God.)

"I'm the only one in the shop who will even do religious stuff on people, you know," Ryan tells me in a way that seems like he wants me to be grateful, after I write out for him what I want him to carve. I nod as if to say thank you, but decide against asking why. I don't need him to explain. I don't want him to explain. I just want him to do this thing with the hot needle and get it over with.

He starts in and I grit my teeth, like I remember doing before, but this time harder because it hurts more. The words take shape as my upper lip begins to sweat. Ever so slightly, I crane my head to the right to look at the man with the dragon shoulder. The buzzing is loud, and he is smiling. *He has a long way to go*, I think to myself, *and I'm almost done*.

I look down at my wrist now, which is still stinging but free of the needle. When I first see the work my eyes well up with tears. Ryan doesn't notice, and I'm glad. *He won't understand what this means*, I think to myself. *He can't know, because no one but God really does.* I'm no middle-aged woman who desires to blend in with the culture by getting a tattoo. No, I'm a middle-aged woman who has spent most of my life being ashamed of God and I'm passionate to wear the change on my wrist.

ROMANS 1:16

"I am not ashamed of this Good News about Christ. It is the power of God at work, saving everyone who believes."

It's a beautiful verse for anyone, but for me, it holds particular significance. To me it means I will never again be timid about God. It means I will never again, like Peter, say I love Him but deny our bond the first time I'm pushed. It means I will never choose the opinion of people over an extravagant, loving, always-been-there-for-me God. It means I will always wear Him, loud and proud in ink on skin that I cannot take off.

And there's a reason this is a big deal to me. A reason besides the obvious.

It starts for me back in high school when an endearingly obnoxious, bleached blond, spiky-haired speaker comes to our church preaching God and peddling T-shirts. I peruse his T-shirt table on the way into youth revival. I have no business buying one with my daddy's money since I own a slew of them from youth camps and revivals already—none of which I ever wear.

But still, it is a different preacher and there are new T-shirts to buy. His T-shirt table houses several intriguing options, from *God's Last Name Ain't Dammit* to the more subtle *God Is an Awesome God*. I reach for neither.

My eye eventually rests on a white shirt with bold shades of blue and green, which will fit in nicely with my '80s mostly Benetton wardrobe. The band music begins to play and I know it is my cue that the gathering is about to start, so without another thought I grab up the T-shirt, pay with my daddy's money, and stuff my purchase under my arm to find my seat. The blond, spiky-haired guy preaches, I go home, I toss the new shirt onto the back of a chair, and I jump into bed and drift off to sleep.

It is two nights later that I plan a mall date with my closest friend. I am in my closet, minutes away from her arrival, desperately looking for something to wear, when I turn to see my new shirt lying on the chair. *It's new,* I think. *And I like the colors.* I pick it up, pull it over my head, and promptly turn to look in the mirror. I'm pleased, at first, with what I see. It's flattering. The colors are good. But this is where my pleasure stops, since in the next second I read the scrolling words in black, smack dab in the middle.

I am not ashamed of the gospel.

Romans 1:16.

And…I panic.

I can't wear this shirt.

Because if I do, people might make fun of me. They might think me a spiritual zealot. They might call me a prude and not include me in fun things. They might ask me if my father is a pastor and say what everyone says when they find out: "Well, you know what they say about preachers' kids." They might tease me for going to that small Christian school instead of the big public one that cooler kids go to, making me feel silly.

I just can't risk it.

So the T-shirt goes back on the chair. And I wear something else.

Before I know it, Wednesday night comes and I am in the great closet search. But this time when I peruse my room and my eyes rest on the T-shirt I am ready. I'm going to wear it tonight because it is safe. I will be at church with lots of good Jesus people, and they will not make fun of me or ask me if I'm a preacher's kid since they already know. They will not think me a prude or call me a zealot. They will be proud of me because I am loudly proclaiming my Jesus on my shirt, and I will feel better about last Friday night when I wasn't willing to.

So I wear the T-shirt. And I go to youth service. And it feels good and like I have, in some way, proven to God that I can be *out* for Him and not have to apologize for it.

And as the night takes over and I find myself back at home and in my bed, my mind questions why I only pick God at church. I think about how I am not afraid to fight for my own rights, but I am panic-stricken at the thought of fighting for Him. And as my body forms to the bed and those thoughts settle in, I mourn the fact that I cannot ignore: I am, in fact, ashamed of the gospel.

I lie there in library-level silence, thoughts flying between head and heart, aware anew that I am in His presence, and He is big. I fear Him, not in that *scary guy in a mask holding a chainsaw coming after me* way, or even in that way my father suddenly looks ten feet tall when I come home late from a date and he's waiting up and I don't want to face him. It's not even that. I'm aware: aware of my sin, aware of my irreverence, aware that I have grieved the Father by not associating with Him. And it's not about a silly T-shirt. It's about my concern for favor among people that has caused me to carelessly trample on my Father's holiness.

Aware and now grieving, I tell Him and myself under the puffy purple covers, *I will never wear this shirt again until I mean it.* And on the chair it rests until one day, many months later, it finds its way to a dusty garage sale table with a bright yellow sticker on its front labeled *10¢* and someone in the market for a bargain buys it.

This is why, years later…the tattoo. Not to pay penance. But to remember my passion.

Friend, I can only pray to God that you never put on your boots of flesh and walk all over the holiness of God like I did. Yes, I was young. I was a teenager, trying to fit in. But does God really care if we are young but still His and yet do not love Him enough to let it be known?

When we do not choose God over popularity we profess Him on our terms. But that is not how God works. It is not what He instructs. Instead He makes Himself crystal clear in Matthew 10:32-33 when He tells us how professing Him is to go down.

Everyone who acknowledges me publicly here on earth,
I will also acknowledge before my Father in heaven. But
everyone who denies me here on earth, I will also deny
before my Father in heaven (Matthew 10:32-33).

We have to be honest with ourselves about what popularity looks
like for us and how it affects us, because it is a real problem in our soci-
ety and it is only getting worse. I parent teenagers. I see what they are
up against. The generation that comes next needs us to show them
a way different from entitlement, excess, and prideful self-love. Are
we, at this juncture, ready to teach it, when we are still caught up in
it ourselves?

The relationship between us and God is not one we get to customize. When we minimize or shy away from our relationship with Him
to be popular with other people, we reject Truth. God did not go to
the cross for us and die in His perfection so
that we might live without responsibility. He
saves us. We accept that or not. If we accept
the gift He gets to come first. *The end.*

> The relation-
> ship between
> us and God is
> not one we get
> to customize.

Coming first will mean we need to die to
people-pleasing. And our hope to be big will
need to be deflated. And we will need to be
okay with both.

How do we become okay with it when
everything in our warring flesh will scream out to be serviced? We
stop allowing self to be an option. We take people's opinions of us
off the table. We choose Him in the moment when it comes down
to Him or us. And in the next moment, we choose Him again. We
choose the thing that will make our soul well. When we choose God
over the god of popularity we choose a soul that isn't at war—war with
ourselves, war with other people and what they may think of us. This
is peace. This is rest.

But it won't be easy.

And it will never be the flesh's first choice.

Yet it will be driven by what we want, at the very core.

God.

And if we choose anything else? It will show us, like our credit card statements and calendars show us our priorities, that we want other things more than Him.

And if that thought scares us—the thought of being disowned by God if we don't choose Him? Well, that is a good fear. Because it means we understand our relationship with God coming first can't be optional.

Being selfish

There comes a point in time where we must challenge our selfishness to a staring contest and, maybe for the first time, not be the first to look away.

I did this a few years ago after a really hard conversation with God and a subsequent lame attempt at a second opinion.

My husband finds me in my bed with lights on and wadded-up snotty tissues surrounding me. I look up from my mess to the deer-in-the-headlights look I've long seen in the eyes of men who aren't quite sure what to do with a crying woman, and I know I will need to let him into my pain.

"I need to ask you a question," I say to him. And then I feel a strong urge to add, "and I need you to be honest." It is in the latter part I feel I may lose him, as most married women and men know this usually means, *Don't lie to me all the way but also don't tell me the whole truth because I probably can't take it.* I can tell by the way he's looking at me that he is weighing what honesty might mean, scrambling to fix whatever I'm about to tell him is broken. But he knows me. And he knows by my face that this is not a question of whether or not my cooking is always good, whether or not I am often a nag, whether or not my butt looks big in jeans. He knows I am serious.

"Okay," he finally says after a pause. "Ask me."

With the naïve hopefulness of a child who already knows the answer to his question, and with that one moment of insane courage it takes to do hard things, I manage to squeak out the words.

"Do you think I'm selfish?"

God had already told me I was. Back when I was in that soul-cleaning-out time of my life, a time when God radically redecorated every square inch of my insides to a place that finally felt like *home*, I had asked Him to break every stinkin' chain that held me. Ones I knew about and ones I didn't. Hard ones, the kind I could never break on my own. And He showed me *selfish*.

And it hurt as bad as you might imagine. Admitting we are selfish is like checking ourselves into a rehab facility full of pock-faced, street-wise unlovelies whom we can no longer see as inferior because we are right there with them—all in the same mess now.

It hurt so much I wanted a second opinion.

He pauses, but not long. I am thankful, for I am ready to hear what I already know.

"Yes," he says softly. "I think you are selfish."

And as the tears fill to the top of my eyes and the ball that is within my throat threatens to choke me, I begin to weep. I have had many fights with my husband through our eighteen years of marriage. We are both passionate people and we have flung machete words in the air in anger, slicing and injuring, some leaving permanent scars, where the goal was to wound and impale and cause a limp for a while. But this was not one of those moments. These were not *those* words. This was that iron sharpening iron moment God talks about in Proverbs 27:17 whereby a person loves another enough to tell the painful truth. It's like seeing a person caught on the tracks and needing to push her to the ground in order to save her life.

It was not an easy moment. It was not an *I've just been to summer camp and I am riding out the Jesus high.* It was an *I've been in a dark, wet, bat-filled cave with no help in sight for years and someone just showed up with a light and some water, strong arms ready to gently lead me out.* I feel pain, but I feel freedom. Because that's what happens when we are willing to let God break a sharp, spiny stronghold.

And maybe you are like the other people to whom I've told that story—well-meaning people who want to make me feel better and say, "Aren't we really all selfish in some way?" (As if everyone sharing the same sin makes it less serious.) The answer is *yes.* Selfishness is what spearheads our desire to be popular. And this, in turn, affects the cause of Christ.

Selfishness causes pastors to preach words that are palatable—speaking about grace and love and peace but skipping over God's justice and righteousness and jealousy for our affection and, yes, judgment for our sin. Selfishness causes businessmen at work to laugh at crude jokes that high-five someone's sex addiction. Selfishness is the *you can have your burger any way you want it* kind of service that gives people what they want in the moment but sacrifices standard and taste because the messenger doesn't want to be the bearer of bad news to hungry people. It is the antithesis of the Gospel, which is of great heartbreak to God.

And what it says to the generation that comes behind us is crazy scary: *Don't preach truth if it will cause you to seem closed-minded. Don't fight for the cause of Christ when it's not popular. Do things that sell or increase your likability. Become famous so you and everyone else will focus on you. Water down God.*

As long as we are more invested in ourselves than God, we will.

So how do we stop being selfish? We stop going for a second opinion. We own it, to ourselves and to God. We take it on in a staring contest and hold our gaze no matter how uncomfortable it gets.

And the desire for popularity fades in the sight of things being right with God.

Why Not?

Most of us have tried finding our value in the opinions of others, and it hasn't worked. We have scrambled for years, hoping people will like us. We have hunted people down, breathing down their neck for them to give us value. And this is not just a high school problem that we finally outgrow. No. As we get older, we scramble to find relevance before our hourglass runs out. The human desire for acceptance and love is a flood that, without God, never dries.

But what if we spend our entire life trying to please others and get them to like us only to, in the end, find out it was all futile? What if it's true what Solomon found out the hard way, that all the glory of man would be like the wind, which can never be contained?

And even greater still: What if we spend so much of our life trying to pacify the requests of others that we completely miss the voice of God?

The truth is, were we to gain the popularity we think we want, we would in the same space secure the death of our full desire for God. Because human flesh can only worship one person at a time:

> You must worship no other gods, for the LORD, whose very name is Jealous, is a God who is jealous about his relationship with you (Exodus 34:14).

We get to choose. It will be Him or us. When we choose things that are not of Him, by default or on purpose, we choose us. The problem with choosing us is that we humans were not created to handle people worship. We just can't, and we shouldn't expect it. It would be like taking a cup and filling it up past its top and getting upset when it overflowed. The cup simply wasn't made to hold that kind of volume and it shouldn't have been expected to. It's inadequate and limited, and we can see that going in. We are the same way.

We are inadequate and limited and not meant to have the attention turned our way. We are finite vessels, not eternal ones, and we have a penchant for fleshly things. So to ask ourselves to handle people praising us, to be able to accommodate heaps of love and affection that we don't have the capacity to carry without making it about us? It isn't fair. It just doesn't work.

> Were we to gain the popularity we think we want, we would in the same space secure the death of our full desire for God.

He's supernatural. We are not. He can handle our full love, full allegiance, full praise, full heart, and never step on it, misuse it, diminish it, or turn it around to benefit Him. We cannot.

Having been a part of the church and a part of ministry since I was a child, I have seen the sad downfall of passion for God, the rise of human success, and the subsequent crash and burn. I have seen pure and goodhearted young pastors who started out with fire in their belly and raw, guttural passion on their lips rise to a certain level of fame and come crashing down because they suddenly weren't open to counsel anymore. Suddenly they believed in themselves and their abilities more than they trembled before God. And those on the outside who were skeptical of God in the first place now mock the whole God thing because *look what another one of His believers did now*. Hard truth? We are all capable of this.

In our everyday life we have done it too. We have relied on our own abilities, our own successes, our own personalities to attract people to us and throw God in as a part of the package. Then when we mess up, which we always will because we are human, we have to explain to people why even though we claim God we look no different.

So maybe we just stop doing it. Stop expecting people to handle being treated like God and act surprised when they can't. Stop wanting people to treat us like God. Just stay human and let God be Himself.

In the midst of writing this book, I have a very distinct dream. It is one of those dreams that is so random it is not random at all. I've only had a few in my life. But those few, I remember.

I'm in a room with some people—all strangers to me. I hear them talking about me, in front of me, which is weird, and for a few minutes I do not respond. "I hear she has a wrist tattoo," one of them whispers loud enough for me to hear her. "What does it say?" another one wants to know. I walk over to them, clustered in a little group, to show them my wrist so they can read what it says for themselves. But when I do, I look down at my arms to see I have words and notes scribbled all over them. The writing covers so much I can't figure out what my wrist tattoo actually says and strangely, I can't remember. I'm standing in front of the people for what seems like hours, frantically trying to wipe off all the other words, licking my thumb and rubbing hard against my skin, just to get all the other stuff off, but to no avail. I feel foolish and embarrassed, not just because of all the scribble but also because I can't remember what I had tattooed on my wrist and I can see by the way the people are looking at me that they do not believe it is even real.

When I realize I will not be able to wipe all the words off, I leave the room in defeat, going back into the area where I left my purse, phone, and keys. I get there only to discover they are gone. Distraught, I know instantly: Someone has stolen them. As this realization sets in I notice a man standing there, watching me, and I say to him in protest, "They stole my stuff!" And calmly he answers back, "Yes, they did." And I am mad and I yell back at him, breathlessly, "You were standing here the whole time—why didn't you stop them?" Pointedly but lovingly, he says to me, "I tried calling out to tell you, but you couldn't hear me because you were so busy trying to explain yourself to those people so they would understand you."

Friends, we have wasted so many minutes and hours and days and yes, years of our lives trying to explain ourselves to other people, trying to get them to like us, trying to become accepted and popular.

And in the process we have lost things. We have let other people take important things away.

We have even involved people in the intimacies between us and God. We have taken our private relationship public. We have sometimes waved the things between us and God around carelessly, like the bragging rights of a good grade on a test, using God to get people to think we are wise, strong, or worthy.

But at a certain point, we must decide to keep other people out of our relationship with God. We must stop sacrificing the richness with Him. We must understand that what goes on between us and God is not social: It's sacred.

We have to get to the point where we say, "Never again will I scramble or chase anyone who is not God. Never again will I beg someone to believe in what God and I can accomplish together." Because most of the time people won't know. They won't believe. They might be jealous. They may not understand. They can't see it, because they aren't God.

This thing with God is *personal*.

So let's not give that up. Let's not compromise our ability to be honest, authentic, and genuine, because we have to skew truth to pacify people. Let's not settle for life with an imposed agenda—imposed by others who dictate how we will live. Let's not allow our fear or shame or selfishness to win the staring contest. In this area of popularity, let's seek revival.

Revival

We are almost to the end of the chapter, but I need to tell you a few more important truths.

When we let people dictate our value instead of God, we're going to find ourselves…

- bumping into ourselves and blaming God for not using our life when we get in our own way.

- chasing after people who are unable to give us what we need.

- exhausted by the constant campaign it takes to convince people we are worthy.

- dictated to by other people as to how we live, what we say, what we must do.

- living scared, ashamed, or selfish.

- listening to others; missing the voice of God.

When we finally get tired of these things and want God more, revival will come. This is when we will be able to get out of the cave of people-pleasing that is dark and damp and seems hopeless, and we will finally see light.

> Revival fires are birthed in Christ-first hearts.

Revival in the area of popularity will enable us to "be content with obscurity, like Christ" (Colossians 3:4 MSG). This does not just apply to being known or famous. It means we are no longer enslaved to people even if we are content with living a quiet life. The chains come when we live with human opinions coming first. And the idea of being free from them?

Dance-worthy.

Yell-worthy.

Dead things becoming new.

Game-changer.

Huge.

Most of us have never known life this way, but we salivate over it.

Revival fires aren't started by résumés, successes, or nepotism; they aren't fanned by who we know or who starts following us on Twitter. They are birthed in Christ-first hearts. In this way, popularity is not only unnecessary, but a hindrance to revival.

During the Welsh Revival, Evan Roberts heeded the call of God to speak His Word. When Roberts went places to preach, he did not care if he would be well received there. He just went and let God take care of the rest.

He would sometimes preach, though some say he was not even very eloquent, but sometimes he would simply sit and pray and never utter a word. And God, through this spirit of yieldedness, blew in big. If Evan had been about popularity, the Spirit could not have used him in the same way since he would only have been halfway focused on God. He would have tried to make his words perfect. He would have worried about his competition. He would have worried about the opinions of the congregation, ready to hear a word from him and angry when he did not deliver. (I shudder to think what would happen today if a preacher showed up but didn't preach. Would we not complain to others that we didn't get what we came for?)

Roberts was a coal miner who came from a long line of coal miners. Would turning from that into a preacher be a popular choice? Not likely. It was an unknown. It was radical. The climate of that time didn't call for preaching to be successful. Bars were thriving, brothels were in full swing, people were drinking and pleasuring themselves to death and weren't expecting God to blow in and mess all that up.

But through Roberts and others, God moved and moved big. Over 100,000 people were saved. Bars and brothels went out of business.

People stopped showing up for football games—even the players stopped showing up—because they preferred to show up to church and hear from God.

Revival.

We need some of that revival down in our soul. Right where we are, soccer mom or executive dad or pastor or artist or young person or anyone outside or in between. We need God to show up and blow up our lives with His presence.

But first, people will need to get out of the way.

> A person with a changed heart seeks praise from God, not from people (Romans 2:29).

Questions for Reflection

1. In what ways does popularity hinder the work of God in our lives?

2. How is popularity futile?

3. Jeremiah was not a popular speaker and in fact, he preached for 40 years without seeing people change. Does that inspire you, discourage you, motivate you, or help you? In what ways?

4. Why is it so important to know what God thinks about popularity? What important element of this does He talk about in Luke 6:22 and how do we prepare ourselves for that?

5. How has your need for popularity personally affected you?

6. What will you most need to die to before popularity will be taken off the table? Your fear? Your shame? Your selfishness? Name some proactive, practical ways you can help yourself in this area.

7. Do you crave revival in this area of your life? What will that look like for you?

Take Your Own Inventory

1. I think about how people will accept me before I do something God prompts me to do. True / False

2. I base at least 50 percent of my decisions off of other people's input and influence. True / False

3. I have neglected to do things for God because other people didn't endorse it. True / False

4. I quit using my gift when people critiqued it or I felt like it wasn't well received. True / False

5. I have something God has put on my heart for me to do but my fear of what other people will think is currently holding me back. True / False

6. There have been times I have not been completely vocal or passionate about my love and loyalty to God because it wasn't popular to do so at the time. True / False

7. When people praise me I don't feel as much of a need to turn to God to be my strength and comforter. True / False

8. I feel like I can't stop wanting to please people, even though I know my life is not to be about popularity. True / False

9. I tell God He is enough but I still try to get people to like me. True / False

10. I want revival in this area of my life and to be freed from the chains of the opinion of others. True / False

5

I Want God
More Than Blessing

I want God, not my idea of God.

C.S. Lewis

There are people who, when you leave their presence, leave you hungry for God. I can think of no better thing to bring out in another than this.

It is this way for me with Mark and Susie, a couple I have known almost my entire life; Mark, since I was a child. The Mark I know then has thick, wavy brown hair, a Southern drawl on full lips, a renegade spirit. He is a twenty-something with life in his step. My daddy is fond of him, tells him he's meant to be a preacher, maybe because the two are so much alike he recognizes his own reflection. It is no wonder, then, he becomes my eight-year-old crush, second only to my daddy. Mark and his brother, Dan, become surrogate sons of sorts, following my father in ministry from Texas to Missouri, where Mark eventually becomes a youth pastor just weeks after marrying Susie. They become my babysitters when my parents are away; family without the blood. I am barely thirteen when they tell me they feel the Lord's call to go back to Texas, but they never leave my heart, though the years are long before we meet again in person.

Bottom Line

Want God, not what He can do for you.

Nineteen years.

I travel to Texas for a conference a day early to visit them. I see Susie first as she welcomes me into their home—an eclectic mix of vintage chic and Texas tumbleweed charm—and get an immediate sense of story. Every picture on the wall, the deer head over the upright piano, little boy Mark's drawing in a gold frame by the kitchen door…all evidence of a life well spent. Grace and love live here, and I long to stay. And for this reason, too: There is something about people who know where you come from that just feels like home. These are my people.

Susie is beautiful, with a stunning batch of red hair, and we talk with ease. She's asking me about life, writing, the family of mine she sees on Facebook, and telling me about hers. It is sweet, this communion with her, though I find myself wishing it hadn't been so long, already grieving how long, again, it may be. (Which is a vice of mine, by the way—to be thinking of the next moment so as to lose the joy of the one I'm in.) After several minutes, Susie walks me into the kitchen. I watch and we talk while she cuts tortilla strips to garnish our simmering dinner, already in progress. It is where Mark finds us when he arrives home.

He busts through the kitchen door, wraps his arms around me, and plants a kiss on my cheek. "Mark!" is all I can really say, for words are not enough. I'm suddenly eight again, and he's twenty. He knows about the gap in my teeth, my Dorothy Hamill haircut, my brother, my church, my daddy and my mom, and for that, I love him.

We sit down to dinner, piping hot soup and cornbread, all made with love in Susie's kitchen. I am wondering how she has read my mind; how she knows that a cup of soup can feel like Jesus to a traveler's weary bones. But this is her life and Mark's: hands and heart, serving up God. It's who they are, so they just *know*.

Over soup Mark talks, filling in time gaps, telling me things I don't know about the 19 years since I've seen them: about the churches, the ministries, the places, people, things, and God. He talks of the hard times, the faith, the necessary endings that break relationships and hearts, the journey that has them looking back with gratitude for it all. He tells the story of when their young son is small and wants a cookie from Wendy's for 48 cents, which they literally do not have. They are between incomes, living in another family's home on a salary of faith. Somehow Mark scrounges up enough change to buy his son a cookie. It is a low moment in his life, wondering where God is, if He sees him, if He really is Jehovah Jireh, the God who provides.

The next day, as he goes to the gas station to get fuel for his car on the bit of money he has saved, Mark looks down to see a penny. Low in spirit, he physically bends to pick up the shiny coin, only to hear in his heart the voice of God. *As long as you are humble enough to pick up a penny, I will always take care of you.* This moment is one of the many in Mark and Susie's life where God comes near.

I leave Mark and Susie's house the next day after sleeping like a baby in their guest room. My heart is full: joyful from my time with them, sad to leave. But I am excited since Mark tells me he is coming through Charlotte with a three-hour layover on his way home from a week-long relief effort in the Philippines in just a few weeks. It is a part of what he and Susie do in their everyday life and ministry to the inner city of San Antonio: care for people, offer themselves up to help meet needs. I feel grateful to get to see him again on his way back from such a mission, and so soon.

Two weeks later we meet again at the Charlotte airport. Mark loads into the car, greets my family for the first time, and we take off to grab a bite to eat. (I forget to tell my sons he has earrings, which will tell them that even a gray-haired guy can be cool, but I see they notice them anyway.) He's tired, with dark half-moons under his eyes, but those eyes still speak life. At dinner, somewhere between the drinks and the nachos, he gets his silver computer out and begins a time of show and tell: showing the pictures, telling the stories of his time in the Philippines after the recent, devastating hurricane…what he saw that broke his heart and the God who showed up in the blackness and rubble. He tells of sleeping on the concrete floor and prayers over the mayor and what it's like to go to a foreign country with no more than a contact name and a phone number and inexplicably receive provision anyway.

It's all real. It's all moving. It's all God.

And as I look at this man across the table from me—this once-young man whose brown, wavy hair has turned shades of silver—I think to myself, *He is a rare collector of God stories.* This man has no wealth or prestige. He teaches inner city boys to play basketball. He travels to foreign places to do good work. He doesn't own expensive cars or carats of diamond jewelry, but he has God stories, and a lot of them. He and Susie are not famous and do not take big conference stages where people love them just because of their name. But they are intimate with God. They serve humbly, and so, making good on His promise the day of the penny, God has always kept them in His care.

And as Mark shows and tells and we eat and listen, all I can see is fruitful labor. And love. And joy, and grace, and God.

And it makes me want Him.

What If We Have It Wrong?

Every once in a while, how much the world has gotten to us shows.

When we hear from missionaries who travel to foreign places with no running water, mud for a floor, roofs that couldn't provide shelter for as little as a mouse, we think how our biggest frustration is our phone charger cord not being long enough to reach the table next to us or the waiter not putting enough ice in our drink or the ten extra minutes we have to sit in traffic because it's rush hour and everyone is trying to get somewhere. And all of a sudden we get how entitled we are. We see it in a flash and it makes us ashamed: We have been dying a slow death by the odorless, colorless carbon monoxide of cushy first-world living. We have no tolerance for real problems, no concept of real blessing.

We look at people who are well-off by the world's standards—lots of money, nice house, attractive spouse, talented kids, prestigious job—and decide they are blessed because the outside symptoms tell us so. We model our lives after them, envy them, put them on a pedestal, because the world has convinced us they are the ones living the good life we all want. We have an expectation of what blessing from God looks like, and it's based on a skewed idea that blessing is *seen*.

Part of the reason we have misunderstood blessing, relegated only to *that which can be seen*, is because of our tendency as believers to be assumers. We assume the blessed are the famous and wealthy because our human standards of worth involve popularity and excess. We assume that when someone does not have such outward bounty, they have done something in their life that made God withhold blessing. When my husband, who has a master's degree and the strongest work ethic I have ever seen, lost his job when we were in our early thirties, people would often ask us, "What do you think God is trying to teach you through this?" in a way that felt like judgment. It suggested we were operating in a way that didn't please God, so He let the rug be pulled out from under us to get our attention and shape us up.

Yes, God sometimes uses hard things in our life to get our attention. And He is always sovereign and always has a plan and purpose and can make good from bad and teach lessons, even from things He does not ordain but allows. But it is not a matter of *we are good so we are blessed* or *we are bad so we are not*. Life is hard, and God's blessing goes beyond what we can see.

We also have the tendency as believers to be over-users. We use the phrase "God told me" to cover for mistakes of our own making. We tell people "I'm praying for you" to fill the uncomfortable space when a need is presented. And we use the word *blessing* to support what we see on the outside as the God-favored life.

But the truth is, God's blessing is on a spiritual level, not driven by the measurement of this world. Blessing does not always come in looks or wealth or even health. Instead, God gives us the true bounty our life needs. He details this spiritual level of blessing in one of the most famous passages of the Word, Matthew 5:3-11:

> God blesses those who are poor and realize their need for him, for the Kingdom of Heaven is theirs.
>
> God blesses those who mourn, for they will be comforted.
>
> God blesses those who are humble, for they will inherit the whole earth.
>
> God blesses those who hunger and thirst for justice, for they will be satisfied.
>
> God blesses those who are merciful, for they will be shown mercy.
>
> God blesses those whose hearts are pure, for they will see God.
>
> God blesses those who work for peace, for they will be called the children of God.
>
> God blesses those who are persecuted for doing right, for the Kingdom of Heaven is theirs.
>
> God blesses you when people mock you and persecute you and lie about you and say all sorts of evil things against you because you are my followers.

These verses are a beautiful reminder of how our relationship with God works. He promises blessed things for the one who seeks Him first. It isn't easy to live with mercy, be humble, and work for peace. Christ calls us to do hard things in a carnally combative world—things that are only possible through Him. We will do them when and only when His good things become our preference.

But He expects some things of us, too. We realize our need for Him. We are humble. We crave justice. We are merciful, pure, and work for peace. We do right in the name of God. None of these things involve the rat race of life, getting the right degree, doing something to become famous, choosing the right neigh-borhood to live in. Instead, He talks of spiri-tual things manifested in our everyday life because of our ultimate desire for Him. We honor God with our character, and the people in our life get to know Him through us.

> Blessing does not always come in looks or wealth or even health. Instead, God gives us the true bounty our life needs.

And then, the best part: the blessing. But again, not necessarily in the world's terms, though many of the things He promises are, in fact, what every soul hungers for. He doesn't say, "God blesses those who go to a good school and pick the right career with a job that can't ever be lost. God blesses those who are good-looking and athletic with good-looking and athletic kids. God blesses those who appear perfect and do everything right with a perfect life." Instead He says, "If you honor Me and make Me most impor-tant, I'll give you My good things. I'll provide comfort when no bed is soft enough to lay your broken heart on. I'll help you live fulfilled, even when you have little of earthly value. I'll see that you're shown mercy, called My child, inherit the earth and the Kingdom of Heaven, and then, on top of all that, the *coup de grâce*: You'll see Me." These are the things that make our life rich. Not the house, not the prestige, not even the family. But the true, lasting, good things of God that make us able to live in a difficult, fickle world.

This, my friend, is blessing.

When we say we want God more than we want blessing, what we really say is, *God, Your goodness over anything else I feel, taste, touch, or see.*

It's a part of spiritually growing up.

Growing Up

A child wants what he or she wants now.

It is a self-centered approach: *This looks good and I'm entitled to it, right here and right now. I need something and will do what I need to do to get it.* When we are babies who don't really know God, it's our approach, too.

My pastor, Jay, talks about this in a recent sermon. He talks about how often, we treat God like a vending machine. We push the buttons we want and expect Him to produce. I think about this and about my freshman year of college, when on more than one occasion my girlfriends and I slip into the laundry room when it is dark and our dorm mates are sleeping. Being young and silly, we stick an opened coat hanger up in the vending machine to see if we can snag something we want for free. It's all a game, really, to see what we can get for nothing. I think about how I sometimes do this with God: I want to receive His goodness without doing my part. *How selfish*, I think to myself. *Time to grow up.*

But this is not the only way I treat God, and Jay's illustration reminds me. He's still talking about this vending machine thing—about how we never show emotion to a vending machine when it's producing. It's a normal interaction of give and receive that leaves us feeling like the contract is good. We got what we want and we can now walk away. But on that one occasion when the vending machine does not produce what we want? It becomes the target of our angst.

"What a rip-off!"

"It took my money but didn't give me what I want."

"This stupid thing."

"I got gypped."

And we pound our fists on the machine, trying to get the money or the product to come out. We shake it, we cuss at it, we push the coin return until our finger hurts because we want what we want and we want it now. This is the most emotion we ever show toward a vending machine—when we do not get what we want.

Don't we also do this with God? Shake our fists at Him when what we expect out of life doesn't happen? Don't we go through life half-heartedly until we don't get what we want? And then and only then does our passion come out—a passion that fights for our comfort and taste and rights. Won't we often much more quickly fight for our rights and wants than fight for God things—those things of the Beatitudes God promises to bless?

We act like children. We put God in the red suit with a white beard and jump in His lap and tell Him all the many things we want. We are so busy rattling off our list, in fact, that we don't even notice He is grieved. We are His children, yes, and He wants good things for us. But He is looking for us to get past the "what can You do for me" place to the "what can You do through me" place where He can show us the true meaning of blessing.

Wanting God more than we want blessing is a sign we are spiritually growing up. It doesn't mean we don't want our life to be good or we assume that along with God will not come good things. He makes it clear in the Word that walking with Him is accompanied by blessings. It simply means that we want Him and not the shiny packages we think He may bring us. We commune with Him, not just when we are asking Him to give us what we want. Our passion for Him is full-time, not just when He comes through for us in the way we think He should. Wanting God more than blessing means if He never does another thing for us outside of dying in our place on the cross, that is *enough*.

Have you ever stopped to think that maybe the reason we don't want God in that passionate way we see others wanting Him is because we have relegated Him to a mere producer for our needs…and this is only a part-time job?

God doesn't want to be our part-time producer. He doesn't want us to talk to Him only when we have something we need or want. And He knows, even without our admission, when this is the case with us. The only cure for such hypocrisy is a heart that truly wants Him first.

It's really the key to everything.

The Part of Blessing That's on Us

At this point, I know what you may be thinking.

But Lisa, shouldn't we want the blessing of God? After all, Jabez asked for it, point blank, in 1 Chronicles 4:10 when he said, "Oh, that you would bless me and expand my territory! Please be with me in all that I do, and keep me from all trouble and pain!"

Please hear me say this: Wanting God's blessing is not wrong. Asking for God's blessing is not wrong. In His name, on His terms, it is *right*.

And the truth is, sometimes God's blessing *is* visible for other people to see. When Abraham's servant went to speak to Laban about getting Rebekah for Isaac's wife, he described his master, Abraham, by his outward, tangible blessings:

> "I am Abraham's servant," he explained. "And the Lord has greatly blessed my master; he has become a wealthy man. The Lord has given him flocks of sheep and goats, herds of cattle, a fortune in silver and gold, and many male and female servants and camels and donkeys" (Genesis 24:34-35).

God is a God of blessing. Remember: He *loves* us. And we want to give beautiful things to those we love.

But if the litmus test for God's blessing is the physical and material, how then can we explain those who want Him first, seek Him first, and have right and undivided hearts toward Him, but have very little by the world's standards? If this were the symptom of God's blessing, then we would be able to tell who was a God-server and who wasn't by mere affluence. If this were the case, I know a lot of godly people who would not be included. Is the favor of God not on the poor?

And then there would be those churches—the quieter ones that aren't as popular as the megas—that would not be seen as having God's favor if blessing for a gathered body were relegated to numbers. And yet good work goes on there, too. Is God not blessing that worship place?

When we look at it like this the thought seems silly. But often even in our subliminal minds we believe that blessing is what is *seen*. We see a church grow and get widespread attention and we automatically assume it has God's favor on it. We see a person become famous and we automatically ponder what they have done right that we have not to be in that place. We see a family experience a heartbreaking loss or hardship and we secretly assume there is something in their life that is not right with God and He's trying to get their attention.

But what if we have it wrong?

If we could predict or choose our own blessing based on our limited human minds, we would ask for things that weren't good for us and deny things that didn't look pretty but would wind up being among the best of our lives. It's just in our nature to not know what we really need.

Blessings from God do not come just because we want them.

Blessings from God come as a result of first wanting Him and then enjoying the goodness that is part of His promises and character.

There is no doubt: Walking with God *does* bring benefits. He says it Himself in Psalm 103:2. "Let all that I am praise the LORD; may I

---

never forget the good things he does for me." But saying God blesses us by making us wealthy is misrepresentative of what it really says in the Word. God knows what we need; we do not. He sees up ahead; we can't. And we either trust Him to be sovereign and know all, even when we cannot make human sense of it, or we don't. Some blessings will not look like blessings. We need God to decide what a blessing for us really is.

Psalm 103:3-5 reminds us what some of those blessings are:

> He forgives all my sin
> and heals all my diseases.
> He redeems me from death
> and crowns me with love and tender mercies.
> He fills my life with good things.
> My youth is renewed like the eagle's!

All of these things are of the supernatural, not the natural: none of which can be measured in human terms. Even the part about "heals all my diseases," which we tend to interpret as meaning *if we get physically ill He will heal us,* is somewhat intangible. We know from Scripture that not every person who was dedicated to God but had some physical ailment got better. Timothy had frequent illnesses (1 Timothy 5:23) and Paul lived with a "thorn in the flesh," likely something painful and chronic (2 Corinthians 12:7-10; Galatians 4:13). Even David, who may have written the very words "[The Lord] heals all my diseases," had an infant son who became sick and died (2 Samuel 12:15-19).

> Some blessings will not look like blessings. We need God to decide what a blessing for us really looks like.

Were we to measure those things in human terms, God did not

keep His word. And yet, as we know from Scripture, we receive the fullest measure of healing when we get to heaven, not while we are here on earth (Isaiah 35:5-6; 2 Corinthians 4:17-18; Revelation 21:3-4). In that way, complete healing is still in our future.

Wanting God more than blessing means that while we are grateful to align with a God of good things, we want Him just because He is God. This is wanting God with a pure heart. Otherwise, how is wanting God to help us get ahead in life any different from wanting another *person* to help us get ahead?

Yes, walking with God brings blessing, so naturally it will be a desire of ours to want the things only being a child of God can bring. I am grateful, every day, for my association with the One who holds the keys to the universe, who has the power to speak words and start life and the same power to shut it all down. I'm no dummy: I want to be on the side of the power; I want to be under the care of someone Great. We all do.

But wanting Him more than His blessings means that He is great enough already—He doesn't have to prove His greatness anymore. When we want God first, we will not be preoccupied with the things He might then do for us; we will be focused on Him and able to enjoy those blessings that come with aligning with Him.

Abraham, for example, was not blessed because he was a great guy. He was blessed because he lived a life of faith. He wanted to obey God first, and by so doing, put himself in a position for God to both use him and bless him. And though his outward blessings were great, the things he experienced God do through him far exceeded it all. In the end, he didn't just have a bunch of cows and money. He had an amazing collection of real-life God stories. He fathered an entire nation of people. He walked intimately with God, which made him blessed indeed.

And isn't this what we really want, friends? To know that our life will matter beyond what we do here? Is living the God adventure not the real blessed life?

Every other blessing we have here on earth has an expiration date. Why, then, would we want the temporal blessings of earth, if just to feel important for a few years or have a lot or get to drive a shiny new car that will, like everything else, one day get old and rusty? Could it be that we need some higher standards?

We miss the blessing of God when we make it about the blessing. We receive the blessing of God in the fullest sense when we make it about Him. Sweet, sometimes intangible, invisible to the naked eye, but always, always, complete. Many people have chased the world's definition of blessing (money, success, good looks, power) and have gotten into trouble. But wanting God will be one chase that will never need maneuvers or angles and won't carry with it empty promises or contingencies. It will never require manipulation or stepping on anyone in the process. It is a pure, unadulterated pursuit, and it will never, ever be wrong. What other aspect of life has this guarantee?

God wants to bless us. We are His loves, His children, and when there is a good gift on this earth it is from Him. He wants us to know blessings now so we will have a tiny taste of all we will enjoy in a perfect, untarnished life in heaven. Here, we have a little. There, we have it all in the full. He blesses us with spiritual fuel to keep going when it's hard and provides sweet springs of spiritual water in an otherwise desert world. If there are blessings for you on this earth, friend, they are no accident, so drink them in.

When it comes to blessing, as with everything else, God is looking for the relationship with Him to come first. We don't use God to get what we want. Instead, we have the kind of relationship with Him where we can ask Him for anything. No request is too big or too out there. His heart and hands are open to the ones who He knows have already proven themselves to be faithful to Him.

Which brings me to back to Jabez and his prayer. You should know: Jabez was not some fly-by-night God follower who went to summer camp, got caught up in the conviction, and made a bunch of empty promises to follow God when he went back home that didn't last for more than a week. Scripture tells us he was a praying man—one more honorable than his brothers (1 Chronicles 4:9). Yes, Jabez prayed and specifically asked for God's blessing. But what he asked for were good, godly things.

Bless me. (God wants to bless His children.)

Expand my territory. (God wants to expand our influence for Him.)

Be with me in all I do. (God wants to be near us always.)

Keep me from all trouble and pain. (God wants to spare His children, which is why He gave His life on the cross.)

These requests of Jabez were not selfish requests. They weren't from a place of wanting God to be a spiritual Santa—they weren't from someone who didn't really have time for God until it came time to sit in His lap with a list. They were requests from the heart of a man in deep covenant with God, believing with all faith that no request is too big or outlandish and God has the power and ability to do it all. This is the posture from which we must also ask God for things.

But this is where we often miss it. We want blessing because it feeds a human desire. This is not the kind of blessing God ordains. With Him, blessing is an accompaniment to the dedication. He wants us to want Him first, cultivate the relationship, and then ask Him for the world.

It's where amazing God stories begin.

Revival

Revival is preceded by *positioning.*

This is important for us to know, we who are no longer satisfied with our souls being temporarily stirred but never changed. Much of the way God moves in revival is kept tucked within His sovereignty.

Only He knows the moment He will say yes to a prayer, sweep into a gathering of believers, and spiritually explode a city. God moves every second of the day, largely unknown to His people. The God-movements called revivals don't happen every day, though. But one thing is for sure: It will begin with our positioning.

When our family visited New York City last spring, I was taken aback by how different the city looked based solely on where I was standing. Our hotel was in the heart of Times Square (so touristy, I know), and every time I stepped outside its revolving doors I was met with the smell of hot dogs and sewage. Lights shouted at my eyes. Cabs were so close they threatened to run over my feet. But within walking distance in the other direction there were different things to see. Children playing in a grassy park. Churches with quiet, reverent steeples. Blue sky with happy clouds.

And so, too, the underground world beneath me—a city of its own where it's always night. We rode the subway a lot this trip, and every time we climbed the stairs and emerged back into the busy world above I was struck by how different two places of the same city could be. My eyes hadn't changed, but based on where I was standing they saw different things.

This, too, is the place for revival.

When we want God first and most, we position ourselves differently than we did before. Our eyes are the same but see different things. We look at blessings differently, hardships differently, wealth differently, *life* differently. It is why I am not convinced that our focus should be so intent on exposing people to important social causes, but rather helping people fall deeper in love with Jesus. When we come into the world from that position we naturally seek out ways to make it better.

Perhaps the reason we have thus far not experienced a soul revival is because we have not put ourselves in that position. When we focus on a pursuit of God, we automatically position ourselves for greatness. We put ourselves in an environment to watch Him move.

I cannot stress enough how the people of the Welsh Revival of the early 1900s were nothing extraordinary. They just weren't. In all my reading of this move of God, I still only know limited things about a few of the revivalists. The revival affected over 100,000 people, but all it took for God to explode the city was a few people positioned in such a way that God could work through them. And as we know, it had a most powerful result.

Evan Roberts positioned himself in humility through prayer.

Florrie Evans positioned herself in vulnerability by boldly giving testimony in front of others as to what God was stirring in her heart.

The Welsh pastor living in America positioned himself in obedience by leaving one place to go to another, even when to many (including himself) the move did not make sense.

Had Evan Roberts turned back over to sleep when he was awakened in the night by God, had Florrie Evans remained silent instead of standing to give testimony of her love for the Father, had that Welsh pastor stayed in America to preach finely orated sermons, the Welsh Revival as we know it today may never have started.

And what God did on a nationwide basis, He first did in these revivalists' hearts. That is the beauty of a relationship with God: It always starts with the personal. God only did corporately what He did first within each of them. It is why we must seek a revival of the soul before we seek a large-scale spiritual awakening. God is about consuming single hearts for Him one at a time and then bringing those hearts together to do something extraordinary. But revival always begins in *one*.

God may want to do something amazing around you but first, He wants to do it *in you*. His heart is for the individual getting well within, because in a group of healed individuals there is power.

In Ezekiel 37, my favorite passage in the Bible, the Lord gives the prophet Ezekiel a vision of what He longs to do for Israel: unite them as a nation and restore them to spiritual passion for Him from their deadness. He shows Ezekiel a valley of dry bones, representing the remains of people who were scattered and dead. It is a picture highly representative of the church today—how we have gotten to a place of spiritual deadness and how even in that place, God wants to restore to us spiritual vitality, passion, and life.

> The Lord took hold of me, and I was carried away by the Spirit of the Lord to a valley filled with bones. He led me all around among the bones that covered the valley floor. They were scattered everywhere across the ground and were completely dried out. Then he asked me, "Son of man, can these bones become living people again?"
>
> "O Sovereign Lord," I replied, "you alone know the answer to that."
>
> Then he said to me, "Speak a prophetic message to these bones and say, 'Dry bones, listen to the word of the Lord! This is what the Sovereign Lord says: Look! I am going to put breath into you and make you live again! I will put flesh and muscles on you and cover you with skin. I will put breath into you, and you will come to life. Then you will know that I am the Lord.'"
>
> So I spoke this message, just as he told me. Suddenly as I spoke, there was a rattling noise all across the valley. The bones of each body came together and attached themselves as complete skeletons. Then as I watched, muscles and flesh formed over the bones. Then skin formed to cover their bodies, but they still had no breath in them.

Then he said to me, "Speak a prophetic message to the winds, son of man. Speak a prophetic message and say, 'This is what the Sovereign Lord says: Come, O breath, from the four winds! Breathe into these dead bodies so they may live again.'"

So I spoke the message as he commanded me, and breath came into their bodies. They all came to life and stood up on their feet—a great army.

Then he said to me, "Son of man, these bones represent the people of Israel. They are saying, 'We have become old, dry bones—all hope is gone. Our nation is finished.' Therefore, prophesy to them and say, 'This is what the Sovereign Lord says: O my people, I will open your graves of exile and cause you to rise again. Then I will bring you back to the land of Israel. When this happens, O my people, you will know that I am the Lord. I will put my Spirit in you, and you will live again and return home to your own land. Then you will know that I, the Lord, have spoken, and I have done what I said. Yes, the Lord has spoken!'"

From no hope to hope. From death to life, from stagnancy to passion...what God did in this valley of death He wants to do in our churches, communities, homes, and hearts today. We are a people scattered and battered by life. We lie hopeless. We are numb and we are stale. And in this space, He is bigger. Oh, the blessing of being aligned with a God who can truly do something about our haggard state!

And how beautiful that God can accomplish this revival both together and one by one. Though the bones were lying corporately in a valley, they were brought back to life singularly. Church, what if this were us? What if we let God bring the revival to us individually and we joined up as "a great army" (Ezekiel 37:10)?

This is us. We *are* the great army. We are just wounded individuals, some content to stay on the ground, some too fearful to get up, but all needing the same revival. Breath is what He longs to breathe into us: the powerful, lasting, supernatural breath of life.

The blessed life is the one where we live in a constant state of revival. Because we are human, the tendency toward dry bone living is within us all. We will have times in our lives when we will need God to renew us. This is not a shameful thing to admit. It is a powerful, life-changing thing to acknowledge and ask God to change us. The only person who will never get better is the one who never asks God for help.

We won't always be here on this earth, but right now, we are.

So while we are still here, shouldn't we be alive?

Shouldn't we want more for our life than just being content to lie as sinew and bone in pieces on the ground, tolerating our deadness?

Shouldn't we live in the place where God is our greatest want, our spirits creaking only for Him?

It's time to stop self-medicating, stop pretending. Without a doubt, our state is desperate. In life we have only Him.

We need revival of each of our souls. We need to want Him most.

Keep reading. I'm about to tell you how we can.

Questions for Reflection

1. What do you think of when you hear the word *blessing*?

2. Do you believe that the world's definition of *blessing* has usurped God's? If yes, how so?

3. "God's blessings are about more than what we can see." What does this mean to you?

4. What does spiritually growing up have to do with this idea of blessing?

5. If it's not about trying harder or being perfect so God will bless us, what *is* the part we play in this area? Why is that so important?

6. What does positioning ourselves have to do with revival and how does this relate to blessing?

7. Do you want revival in this area of your life? What will that look like for you?

Take Your Own Inventory

1. If I'm honest, I want what God can do for me more than just wanting Him. True / False

2. I base at least 50 percent of my decisions on how much I will be blessed. True / False

3. I have done things for God so He would do something for me in return. True / False

4. I have neglected to do things for God when I didn't know the payoff. True / False

5. I get mad or lose faith when God doesn't bless me like I think He should. True / False

6. Things in my life don't change because I have been stuck in the same position. True / False

7. I often resent other people who appear to have more blessings than me. True / False

8. I make assumptions about how God should come through for me. True / False

9. God is not as vibrant in my life as He could be because I'm too focused on what He will do for me. True / False

10. I want revival in this area of my life and to be freed from being blessing-driven. True / False

6

I Want God
Most

You must love the LORD your God with all your heart, all your soul, and all your mind.

MATTHEW 22:37

Before I start writing this book, I start shopping.

It's summer, that glorious time when my kids' legs are tanned from outside play, grill smells live in my nostrils, and I dive deep into Mommy waters while the writer sleeps by the pool. I like to shop, and when the writer is asleep I seem to shop more. But really, it's about something else: Sometimes I don't want to hear from God, and shopping helps with that.

I think, and I know, that this moment is not about the shopping (because it rarely is). I recognize it as the human impulse of storing up, controlling my world before He starts requiring something of me. When you know God in that intimate way, there is an understanding that when He calls, it will be loud. And it will be specific. And it may require other things to go away. And it's terrifying. So I shop.

But even as I sit in the parking lot of this antique mall with all my precious finds perched around me, I know it is a myth, the storing up. For a brief moment, the

Bottom Line

Remember. Repent. Repeat.

147

shopper subsides and the writer awakens. I take out my phone and go to my notes and the fingers start running and running fast.

> It's all a myth. Chasing this kind of more only brings the foggy high and runs up the bills, and in the end it is the same choice as it was yesterday: out of life, what do I want the most? (That is the question. That is *always* the question.)
>
> But in the meantime, the shopping has gotten almost weird and manic—like I am ravenous for change. I feel the change coming, the unraveling that happens when I start writing a new book and mostly, I want Him to change me but the house is screaming so loud for me to pay it attention instead that I am nearly going deaf. In its every square foot I see imperfection and I want to make it beautiful, and it already is.
>
> I shop because it helps me forget I may never do the *everything* for God both of us want. And the reality of that feels painful.
>
> But no matter how much I shop, I will never be able to muffle Him.
>
> Because He haunts me. Yes, haunts. Not in the creepy, scary movie way where it's about some broken-down clapboard house with squeaky floors and curtains of cobwebs and that guy who died who now lives under the house and occasionally emerges wearing a mask. He haunts me in the unrequited love kind of way whereby you love someone so much it aches and their scent doesn't go away no matter how much you try to scrub it off yourself.

So in the end, after the shopping, I will come back to the same. I'll just have less money.

What I'm really wanting is not to tear my house apart and put it back together more beautifully, but what I want God to do to me: deconstruct me, clean me up, make me better, streamlined, more beautiful. And at the same time I'm scared He will.

This is the rub of my life.

The words are now done and the writer goes back to sleep. I have dialogued with no one in particular, but I have somehow worked it all out.

1. God is what I want most.

2. Other things will scream for my attention.

3. I will have to choose between them.

It is the same for you.

Like Them

Months later I sit at my desk, tasting hot tears that have dripped recklessly onto my lips.

The man on YouTube whom I hear but can't see, David Wilkerson, is preaching the sermon "A Call to Anguish." The strong woman dam inside of me has broken, and I am undone.

He is using pointed words in an old-man voice, and I am consumed with them, and Jesus.

"There is going to be no renewal, no revival, no awakening until we are willing to let Him once again break us."

I gulp hard and try to take this in one swallow, but the words get stuck in my throat. That there might be no revival, no awakening, because of my unwillingness…the thought slays me. Yet the deeper part of me knows I must accept it as truth. Because in my normal, daily life I am fearful, sometimes unable to convince myself that the awakening is worth the cost.

It is why we can't base what we do for God on feelings. Because one moment, passion, and the next moment, fear. And yes, maybe *want* could be called a feeling too. But when it comes to God, the want I'm talking about is the kind where the heart is all in, which makes it different.

Jesus says it many times over in the Word. *If your whole heart isn't in it, you and I won't ever work.* When we want more with a whole heart, God is all over that.

My eyes continue to stare at the black screen while the old-man words from Wilkerson come. They come in swift left jabs and uppercuts—the kind that knock teeth from your mouth and send you reeling. I find myself wanting to have the ref ring the bell for a timeout or thinking I should fall to the floor and pretend I'm knocked out, just to get the words to stop…for I feel them, each one, as they settle in.

"We've held on to our religious rhetoric and our revival talk but we've become so passive."

"Does it matter to you at all that God's spiritual Jerusalem, the Church, is now married to the world?"

"All the devil wants to do is to get the fight out of you…So you won't labor in prayers anymore, you won't weep before God anymore. You can sit and watch television and [you and] your family go to hell."

"There's nothing of the flesh that will give you joy. I don't care how much money, I don't care what kind of new house. There is absolutely nothing physical that can give you joy."

I'm fresh out of good, churchy answers.

What I do know is that the world has gotten to us. The church. All of us. And we look scary normal.

I write about Jesus, speak about Jesus, have given my life to the cause of Jesus, yet I am a Bible Israelite. So much so that I read the book of Deuteronomy with eyes peering through fingers, like I do with things I don't really want to see. The descriptions hit frighteningly close to home.

stubborn
unruly
forgetful
halfhearted
fat on life, not godliness

I could pretend this is not true, that I am higher and better than others. But that is just pride. That is just fooling myself. I have every same tendency to forget about God and become stubborn, unruly, forgetful, halfhearted, and fat on life that the Israelites did…and that you do too. But when our life is about holiness, everything changes. And that, my friend, while we are here on the earth, is going to be an ongoing, ever-growing process.

This is the promise Moses gives to the Israelites then and us now about where obedience, living the more life with God, takes us.

> The LORD your God is bringing you into a good land of flowing streams and pools of water, with fountains and springs that gush out in the valleys and hills. It is a land of wheat and barley; of grapevines, fig trees, and pomegranates; of olive oil and honey. It is a land where food is plentiful and nothing is lacking. It is a land where iron is as common as stone, and copper is abundant in the hills. When you have eaten your fill, be sure to praise the LORD

your God for the good land he has given you (Deuteronomy 8:7-10).

Living a life of obedience, love, and trust with God is really living a
life of fullness. Anything worldly we may give up in the process of pursuing more with God will so far pale when we get a glimpse of what He
has to offer, we will be sickened we ever gave it a moment's attention.
The above passage is not just a picture of the Promised Land then; it's
a picture of the Promised Land now. It is a picture of spiritual abundance, provision, and never-ending resources of joy, peace, love, hope,
fulfillment, passion, and security. It is a life of Jesus in the full.

And God knows that when we are experiencing this abundance is
the time we are most at risk. Because right after Moses tells the Israelites all that good stuff about gushing water and olives and honey, he
brings a word of heavy caution:

> But that is the time to be careful! Beware that in your
> plenty you do not forget the LORD your God and disobey
> his commands, regulations, and decrees that I am giving
> you today. For when you have become full and prosper-
> ous and have built fine homes to live in, and when your
> flocks and herds have become very large and your silver
> and gold have multiplied along with everything else, be
> careful! Do not become proud at that time and forget
> the LORD your God, who rescued you from slavery in the
> land of Egypt. Do not forget that he led you through the
> great and terrifying wilderness with its poisonous snakes
> and scorpions, where it was so hot and dry. He gave you
> water from the rock! He fed you with manna in the wil-
> derness, a food unknown to your ancestors. He did this
> to humble you and test you for your own good (Deuter-
> onomy 8:11-16).

We are most at risk when we are not in crisis. It's a cruel irony, I know. When we have what we need and most of what we want, it is our tendency to wreck our life. This was the Israelites' plight. It is ours, too. When we are comfortable, we are in danger.

And in those moments, when we have comfort and attention and abundance, we are not likely to want more of God because we do not readily feel the lack. We may think that chasing more in this life and world is what we want. But we are wrong. And when those things let us down, when we are more damaged than before, we always come back to the One we want more: *Jesus*.

This passage is meant to wake us up. His Word is meant to remind us, over and over again, not to forget God. It's meant to show us our error and guide us back to the place where we can have clear vision for what is really going on in our lives, right in front of us. It is reproof. It is correction. It is the first word, the last word, and every word in between. It is life-giving and life-saving. It is truth, 100 percent. It is *love*. It points the way—spells out in plain words—how to have the most out of life. Be excited: What I'm going to share with you to help you now move forward is as simple, as beautiful, as rich, as promising, as bottom-line gospel as anything you may ever read.

Coming Back, Moving Forward

I am sitting one day with my pastor-father at his home. We have been talking about my passion for this book and the things I want to express in its pages when I notice his eyes glazing over, taking him back to a place he's already been. Without a word he grabs his Bible like I have seen him do many times before. Using the arm of his recliner as the pulpit, he preaches in his living room to only me.

"You know, I preached on this, Lisagirl," he says. "Maybe you would like to hear it?"

Before the yes can even come, he has begun. And the message is so for now, so for this book, it is enormous.

I need to be vulnerable with you, though, before I share it. Having grown up in a very churched, deeply religious situation, I try to stay away from any quick spiritual fixes, any 1-2-3 formulas when it comes to walking out our relationship with Jesus. Part of this is because of what I've seen formulas do to good church people who wind up becoming religiously rigid. Part of it is because I don't think we can place our faith walk in a one-size-fits-all box. Part of it is because I am a crazy rebel and I just don't like doing what everyone tells me to do. And yet I know the value of giving you, the reader, something to take home to chew on, *to do*, though following hard after God can never be encapsulated in three easy steps. We need guidance. We need all the help we can get, really, to chase the *more* we claim we want with God. And yet I resist it because there is that raw part of me that wants to say, "Just read your Bible and pray, ok? You don't need me to tell you anything else."

So I'm not going to give you three easy steps. I'm not even going to give you my preacher-daddy Jim's pastoral position. What follows are 100 percent Word-driven, Word-taught keys to the *more* we want with Him. (Now for that…somebody say *amen*!)

It's from the book of Revelation.

John is swift with the pen, but the red letters tell us God is speaking. Chapter 2 is addressed to Ephesus, the first church of seven to receive a message. We know from research into that time that Ephesus was the "mother" church out of which the other six churches (at Smyrna, Pergamum, Thyatira, Sardis, Philadelphia, and Laodicea) were born. Maybe it's my psychology background, but I like to think of Ephesus as the oldest child in the birth order of the family: conscientious, responsible, and overall good. In fact, this church was so good they were too good for their own good. (Sound familiar, church friends?)

The Ephesians were workers. We know this because God says, "I know all the things you do. I have seen your hard work" (Revelation 2:2). They were toiling, *kopos* in the Greek, meaning they were working to the point of sweat and exhaustion, demanding everything a person has to give for the sake of Christ.

I'm reminded here of the faithful team at our former portable church, Thrive Church, who would load in and out enough sound equipment and pipe and drapery that it was literally like moving in and out of a small apartment every Sunday. Those men worked and sweated. They stinkin' *toiled*. And they did it all because they wanted to serve God with every inch of their physical bodies. The people at Ephesus were those hardworking, sweat-it-out kind of people, and God noticed.

But they were also spiritually strong. They were noted for their patient endurance, for their intolerance of evil men, for their spiritual discernment, and even for just not quitting (Revelation 2:2-3). I read these descriptions and feel as intimidated as the new kid on their first day of school. These Ephesus people didn't play. They were just *good*.

And yet, Jesus was about *more*. Because the truth is, Jesus is not looking for us to serve Him like a robot with an on and off switch. He doesn't want us to wow Him with our short bursts of faithfulness. He is about the deeper, the richer, the most important, the *forever*, the heart, the all the way, in deep, so in love with Him that every other thing in the picture gets cropped out.

I think of all the good people I have known in my church life, and oh, some of them have been so very good. I think of Pat, the faithful servant of God in my growing-up church who wrote me and many other young people letters every birthday for years and years, speaking vision into my heart and affirming my gifts. I think of the foster mom, Colleen, who takes in children who aren't hers and loves them like they are, even though in the end, she knows she likely won't get

to keep them. She bathes them and feeds them and houses them anyway. I think of my own mother who made an impression on me, even
as a young child, as she would leave tracts with gas station attendants
and witness to strangers because of her passion for God. I have honestly known no greater people in all my life.

But to God, it's not about our goodness. In its purest form, service
and good deeds are an outflow of a vibrant relationship with Him, as
is the case with all of the people I just mentioned. But often sneak-
ing up on us, our deeds and work and sweat become just about looking good before God. And good deeds for God are shallow when they
become routine and aren't ultimately about the *love*.

In his commentary on this chapter, John MacArthur writes,

> Despite all the praiseworthy elements in the Ephesian
> church, the penetrating, omniscient gaze of the Lord Jesus
> Christ had spotted a fatal flaw. Though they maintained
> their doctrinal orthodoxy and continued to serve Christ,
> that service had degenerated into mechanical orthodoxy.
> Though at one time they had love, forty years later the
> affection of the first generation of believers had cooled.*

It's true. Sometimes our love for God cools. We don't intend for it
to be this way—we would even say we don't want it to be this and we
will do anything for it to *not* be this way. But many of us, both believers and nonbelievers, have fallen into the *good* trap, which gets in the
way of the love because it becomes about us. "If I only stop spending money I don't have, I will be *good*. If I only go to church faithfully, I will be *good*. If I take my family to the soup kitchen and have
us serve at Thanksgiving, I will be *good*. If I pray more than I used to,

---

* John MacArthur, *Revelation: MacArthur Bible Studies* (Nashville, TN: Thomas Nelson, 2007),
  61.

I will be *good*." But God doesn't agree. And just like He didn't let the good church people of Ephesus off the hook, neither does He let us—because He knows that eventually, being good will sprout arrogance and thereby kill things meant to grow.

> But I have this complaint against you. You don't love me or each other as you did at first! Look how far you have fallen! Turn back to me and do the works you did at first. If you don't repent, I will come and remove your lampstand from its place among the churches (Revelation 2:4-5).

I have to admit, I shake a little in my boots when I read that God has a complaint and see Him using exclamation marks to make His point. It tells me, without a doubt, that He is dead serious about this. He is extremely passionate about us loving Him.

But in His complaint with exclamation points, the Great Teacher gives the most practical, loving three-point sermon anyone could ever deliver. In just one and a half verses, He tells us how to both come back to Him and move forward into the most thrilling, fulfilling, God-centered life. It is all we need to know to start today, this very moment from wherever we sit, having that more life we say we want.

Remember

> You don't love me or each other as you did at first! Look how far you have fallen! (Revelation 2:4-5).

Those poor Ephesians. Just when they were feeling all warm and tingly from God's endorsement of all the glorious work they were doing, He throws them a curveball in the form of a confrontational word. But it is one of the things God does best: assures us He loves us while requiring us to be better. The Ephesians had a memory lapse about the goodness of God they had been shown and what all of their goodness was really all about, and God needed them to remember. It is the same thing we struggle with, humans that we are—to remember God in the moments we aren't in crisis.

In the Old Testament book of Deuteronomy, the Israelites are given no instruction more often than this: *Remember*. It is repeated over and over again, making clear that Israel has been flat-out *forgetful*. All throughout the book God is saying to the people of Israel, "Hey, people! *Remember* when someone once owned you and abused you and I rescued you and set you free? *Remember* those nights you cried out to Me for help and I came through? *Remember* how badly you wanted Me to prove Myself so I performed amazing miracles right before your eyes? *Remember* how strong you needed Me to be and I was? *Remember* how you asked Me for grace when you messed up and I gave it? *Remember* how you once told Me you longed for Me? *Remember* who I am and have been in all the 40 years you've been dealing with a bunch of sand and desert smells and arguments with all those other crazy people you were wandering with?"

God is serious about the remembering, so serious that just as the Israelites are going to enter the Promised Land, He has Moses, Israel's leader, remind them of everything they have been through in the past 40 years. Moses recaps the entire journey through the hard wilderness just so they can have it all fresh in their minds when they go into the place where it will be easy to forget God again. It was their human curse and ours. We are just plain forgetful.

In the everyday moving stream of life, even we who love God the very most get swept up in the rushing current of jobs, parenting, school, carpool, laundry, vacations, and yes, even ministries. As we are numbly floating at a swift pace, it is only the occasional debris—a scary health diagnosis, a relationship wound, an injustice on the

TV news—which obstructs us long enough to notice that we haven't talked to God or paid much attention to Him in quite a while and man, now we sure could use His help moving forward. We want Him to please hurry and get us unstuck so we can keep up with our to-do list. We act like children, stomping our feet and carrying on when He doesn't hurry as fast as we think He should. And we wonder, lying in bed at night staring at the ceiling fan, why God seems to like everyone else better. Our selfishness blinds us to what has become of us as we have drifted down the stream of life: We have turned into Israelites.

And God, who has been the always-faithful Father to us (Psalm 86:15), mourns and weeps that we have moved away from Him to the point our love has become divided, tarnished, *forgotten*. He won't stop being faithful, nor will He stop loving. But He will still *grieve*.

Our moving away from God causes our eyes to be blinded to the things He is doing. Our minds feel entitled to the things He will do. Our hearts are calloused to the things He has already done. It leaves us vacant and waffling and so grossly unfulfilled yet engrossed in the life of our flesh that it takes an act of God to point us back in the right direction.

And so we reach the point we find ourselves at right now, today, where we are willing and ready and longing to *remember*. It's not a hard process, but it does take a heart of purpose. It is at this moment that we pull out our adoption certificate—the day we became joined to Christ by becoming His child. We replay the scene. We remember the sights and the smells. We take in all the love and passion. We hear again the words, "Yes, I choose you." He adopted us and we accepted Him as our Father: This is a mutual joining. The richness in the remembering is about the One we have singled out to commit to: Jesus. He wanted us, but still, we had other options. We could have chosen other gods, since there are plenty in this world to choose from. But we chose Him, just as He first chose us. How special. How sacred.

It is a real, true, lasting love story between father and child. Oh, that we would never forget that or hurt our bond to Him with a wandering heart.

There is a reason I opened this book with my salvation story. It is where my life started. It is where your life started too, if you have accepted His gift of salvation. It is where hope lives, grace lives, beauty lives, goodness lives, joy lives, *love* lives. Should we ever, then, want anything more, when we already have it all?

To be all in with God we must start at the place of *remembering*. Pause now, if you can, and pull out every Jesus memory you have. Make a piece of art, write a poem, start a journal, write down all the history, put the pieces together that form the journey you have had with Him. Leave nothing out. (You can do this in your heart, yes, but there is something about the physical act of writing down, of documenting your love story.) Dwell on your Beloved. Say His name over and over again. Write it on every inch of your paper until no white space is left. Remember, remember, remember. And in that place of remembering, fall in love with Him all over again.

Repent

> Turn back to me (Revelation 2:5).

The Ephesians probably didn't like the word *repent* any more than we do. Maybe it's because it reminds us of buttoned-up stone-faced preachers who wear pocket squares and comb-overs and frown on video games and yell that the world is going to hell in a handbasket and we all need to repent or we'll go to hell too!

But the Ephesians were in the same situation many of us are in, today: They had not only forgotten God, but they had turned from Him and started to look away. It is where all sin is born: when our gaze is no longer on God.

"Turn back to me," says God. I can think of no greater physical act that signals disinterest, disloyalty, or dislike more than to turn our back on someone who is standing right there in front of us. The times that any of us have experienced this have likely stood out in our mind because the moment made us feel devalued. God is not a human; He doesn't sit around whining with hurt feelings like we would in that situation. But He can feel devalued. And when we devalue the God of the universe we cause a serious breach in our relationship.

Repentance is a serious word, but it is not a scary word. God doesn't hold us up by the collar of our shirt with our legs dangling in the air and spit the word in our face like some dogmatic bully who likes to throw his weight around. With all the grace, love, and power He has, He says, "You need to turn back to Me and away from all that mess you've been choosing, because failing to love Me with every fiber of your being is sin."

And that, my friend, is why we repent. That is why we turn back. We may not have even known it, but we have been sinning every moment we haven't given all of ourselves to Him.

During the Welsh Revival there was a very palpable spirit of repentance among the people. It is, in fact, one of the key reasons I believe God's power was so fully on display during that year of 100,000 saved. People came back to God. They told Him they were sorry. They cut out all the mess they had been entangled in and turned away from it. It is well documented that during that year when God radically moved, bars and brothels were literally shut down. They couldn't operate because there was no one there to offer service or be serviced. Horses no longer responded to commands because the four-letter words they were used to hearing had been cleaned out of their owners' mouths. Football matches that had once filled large stadiums were cancelled due to the lack of players and spectators. People just didn't show up. They were too interested in God.

Friends, what if we were too interested in God? What if we became obsessed and consumed with nothing but Him? Things would look different. The church would look different. We would look different.

In the book of Joel, the Lord is calling the nation of Judah to repentance. Like the Israelites, like the Ephesians, like *us,* the people of Judah had become fat and lazy, prosperous and complacent. After the prophet Joel has told them the news that a whole mess of locusts were about to get into their every crack and cranny, he tells them they'd better get their act together. If they don't, some worse junk is about to go down. He then gets down to serious business and tells them this:

> That is why the LORD says,
> "Turn to me now, while there is time.
> Give me your hearts.
> Come with fasting, weeping, and mourning.
> Don't tear your clothing in your grief,
> but tear your hearts instead."
> Return to the LORD your God,
> for he is merciful and compassionate,
> slow to get angry and filled with unfailing love.
> He is eager to relent and not punish (Joel 2:12-13).

Don't tear your clothing… but tear your hearts instead. He didn't want an outward show from them; He doesn't want an outward show from us. Back then, a way of saying *I feel such deep sadness and regret for what I have done* was for a person to tear their clothes; now we offer shallow pittance prayers, bolt up to the church to volunteer or take a Bible Study class, talk to everyone we can think of who isn't God to help us get back in good graces with Him. We just want to do something to feel better. But God was very specific with the posture He wanted the people of Judah to take—not one on the surface, but one deeply dredged on the inside, with Him and for Him only.

Being dredged on the inside: the unearthing of the messy, extra stuff in the bottom of our heart's ocean floor; the stuff that shouldn't be there but through sin has made its way in. This is located and revealed only through thorough investigation and soul searching. If we want more with God, if we are tired and done with our relationship with Him just being okay, our lives will need to be in a posture of repentance. This doesn't have to be in a church service. We don't have to kneel at an altar. Sometimes those places are important for us because coming to God in front of other people helps us be accountable, but it can be done at home, in the car, oh, for goodness sake, it can be in the dang middle of Starbucks for that matter. All that matters is that we put our face to Him and our back to everything else, tell Him we are sorry, and mean it.

And good God that He is, He accepts it, forgives, and moves on.

Repeat

> Do the works you did at first (Revelation 2:5).

On the subject of moving on, we find some Ephesians badly in need of doing just that. While they are so busy being good, they have forgotten the all-important aspect of a vibrant relationship with God: being all about Him. Ironically, moving on with God—having more of Him—will mean going back to the time when they did things from an outflow of passionate love rather than punching-the-clock service. They were working from the beginning, and they were working now. But God noticed a difference. They lost the purity of where they were at first and had settled for simply working on autopilot, resting on their goodness.

We fall into this autopilot thing too. When we first fall in love, meet a new friend, join a team or church, or move into a neighborhood, we typically try really hard. We try to be a good partner, employee, member, neighbor, or friend. We bring cookies to the neighbor's door so they will feel welcomed and we feel responsible and nice. We try to be witty and fun and lighthearted and giving and open and impressive. We care what the other person thinks and it's all fresh and new and exciting and deemed worthy of our extra effort. But give it a little time and we tend to become a bit more relaxed and don't try as hard anymore. It's not that we are bad people. It's just that it's in our nature to put forth a lot of effort up front and then relax.

Some years after my wild and crazy freshman year of college, when I moved far, far away from God, my mother tells me a funny story. She tells me about how during my first month of school at the university, she went to visit me. At the dorm's front desk she met Ms. Carol, a nice white-haired lady who sang my praises for being such a sweet and responsible girl. It made my mom proud.

But several months later, when she visited my dorm again, she had a completely different experience. This time, Ms. Carol's face soured when Mom mentioned my name. She didn't explain anything, but then, she didn't have to. Mothers just *know*. I had fallen out of Ms. Carol's good graces.

Now, telling me about it years later, we are laughing like people do when hard stories are far enough in the rearview to be funny. I take this moment for a lighthearted confession, telling Mom some of the antics that ruined Ms. Carol's opinion of me. The late-night vending machine treasure hunts with coat hangers. The turtle we find by the side of the road and rescue to come live in our bathtub. The night we light makeup sponges on fire and throw them in the sink, setting off the fire alarm in the middle of the night.

Ms. Carol has good reason not to like me anymore. I have gone from Lisa the sweet and responsible girl to Lisa the rowdy, plays-too-much-and-occasionally-steals-vending-machine-snacks freshman. If

I'm honest, I think it was only the first month I tried to make a good impression. Don't we all try hard in the beginning?

And then there's God. He isn't asking us to make a good impression on Him because He knew us when we were mere dust. But He notices when our desire to please Him, honor Him, love Him has waned. He knows when we have turned to autopilot and when we are truly bubbling over the good stuff of Jesus and cannot stop.

Like for the Ephesians, doing the deeds we did at first is about making the effort with God we did when we first met Him, fell in love, and couldn't get enough. It's the opening the car door gesture that a man does when he wants to impress a woman—only we aren't out to impress God. We are out to lean into the role of servant. In the beginning with us and God, it was about the love. And in the end and every moment in between, it has to be about the love too.

If we want more of God, we have to take this step of moving forward, which is going back and doing what we did at first. Maybe that will mean we open a Bible and read it from the literal beginning. Maybe we go outside and find a spot in nature to sit and be quiet before God, like we did when we were kids and just needed fresh air. Maybe we never really got off the ground with God in the first place so we start doing things that stretch us—things we have always secretly wanted to do (or maybe *never* wanted to do) but got scared and shied away from. One thing is for sure: God isn't picky about how we find Him and serve Him. He just wants us to find Him and serve Him.

The Most Life

If I could sit real close and hold your face in my hands I would whisper, *Let's do this thing together.* Because we are traveling close, friends, closer than we think, and it has nothing to do with mere miles. It has to do with the road all of us are traveling down, if we are believers in Christ, that is bumpy and full of stupid potholes we didn't see coming, and yes, twists and turns that sometimes have us throwing our heads back with laughter and other times have us clutching the door handles in fright. This is the truth. This is real life.

And what I can tell you for sure is that tomorrow, I will fail. And the day after that, I may gain some small victory. And the day after that, I may behave poorly or really well. And then I will lay my head down on the pillow and close my eyes until the next day I wake, facing new mercies with the sun or rain or whatever God sends. It is the journey. If only it were simple.

But though it is not simple, *it is sure.* We will be here until He's ready for us to be gone. We will never have a perfect day, no, not one, even when the wind blows at a perfect speed and the air hangs at 68 degrees and we have tasted good food and laughed with loved ones and gone to bed feeling fully in love with it all. On this journey, we will have friends who leave us and ones we meet in our gray-haired years who we are surprised to have lived so long without. We will have moments that seem to last 89,000 hours and ones that go by in a millisecond that we wish to freeze and hold awhile longer. We will dream and some will be silly and some will come to pass. We will find hope in small things, like birds that sing on top of dumpsters and stories from children who grew up in darkness but rise to become lights of the world. We will grow and then, just when we think we are through growing, we will grow some more and it will feel harder. And we will watch ourselves, as through a window peeking in, do that one thing we never thought we could. And though it is much smaller we will feel, just for a moment, like an Olympian or mountain climber or runner who completes a marathon without two good legs because we, too, are overcomers. And then, just as surprising, a new possibility will creep in and we will count the gifts and find ourselves sinking into joy and smiling a little bigger.

And most of all, we will be with God. We will step heel-clacking paces behind a silent step up ahead. We will be cared for, like the Israelites who despite their long travels were reminded by God, "For forty years I led you through the wilderness, yet your clothes and sandals did not wear out" (Deuteronomy 29:5). We will sway to music He orchestrates and even when that music plays too fast or loud for our liking, we will keep swaying because it is innately born within. We will have tears fall that He wipes with fingers we can't see and feel the gift of being cradled without physical hands holding us.

We will be with God. He will be with us.

And then, one day, it will be for real. And the glory of the One who is Everything will be fully in our sight. And all this other mess we have settled for will not be longed for, even if it was our favorite thing to do in the whole wide world, because it won't be Him. And that is the moment we will no longer have to say, *I want more.*

I write these words just minutes before engaging in a mad rummage in my office filing cabinet for something I am trying to find. I am caught off guard when, in my search for something completely different, a card brushes my hand. I have tucked it away in a place I don't often visit because the sight of it makes me cry. It is a card about my friend. Months ago, she died.

Her name was Jennifer, and even as I fight to type the word *was* I know in my head it is so. She made it to the age of 40, which makes me smile because somehow, even though that is painfully short, it feels like she got to be a grown-up. I loved her. I love her. I wish so much she weren't gone.

About six months before she dies, Jenn asks me to do her eulogy. The question comes to me late into the night when she has insomnia, and night owl that I am, I am playing Words with Friends on my phone. *Lisa?* she types. *I want to ask you something but then I never want to speak of it again, ok?* As I read the words, a part of me knows where this is going, and I don't like that sad place. But I feel duty. And I feel love. My fingers type *ok* before I give them permission. Jenn's two and a half years into her battle with cancer, and she is far from giving up the fight, but she's also wise enough to know to make hard plans.

I want you to speak at my funeral, ok? Don't argue with me. Just please say yes. You are who I want to speak. I gulp hard as I read the words. It doesn't take the tears long to fall, for they have for months been held back like racehorses behind a gate, wanting to run. I don't want to hear this talk of funerals. I don't want to think of my beautiful friend going away. I want us to keep texting late every night like we have for two and a half years—keep talking about yoga and the kale shake her husband just made her and how handsome our boys are and what kind of new skincare she's trying out and how, when she gets better, we're so gonna go somewhere tropical for a girls' weekend and celebrate. I don't want to hear the Beaches song playing and replaying in my head or picture myself all in black, standing at a church podium, trying to find words that are worthy of a life because God knows, there just aren't any very good ones then. I want my friend to live. And I don't want to say yes to anything but that.

And yet I know it is not my choice. I know it is in the hands of her Maker, who loves her far more than I. And so, through my fears and my tears, I let gratitude in. Gratitude for the honor of knowing her, for the God who knows best, for being asked to represent her in a moment I know, as a non-family member, I don't deserve. Slowly, purposefully, I type the words I know she is waiting to see. *Yes*, I text simply. *Yes, I will.*

Some months later, after Christmas and the turn of the New Year, Jenn goes home to be with her Jesus. On a beautiful Saturday afternoon, the sun shining bright as if to say *She's all good now*, I find myself standing at a church podium trying to find words worthy of Jenn's vibrant life. So many things I want to say. So little time to say them.

Before I speak the personal words of my eulogy, I read a passage from my favorite book. They are words I have tucked away in my heart for just this moment.

> O Lord, I live here as a fish in a vessel of water,
> Only enough to keep me alive,
> But in heaven I shall swim in the ocean.
> Here I have a little air in me to keep me breathing,
> But there I shall have sweet and fresh gales;
> Here I have a beam of sun to lighten my darkness,
> A warm ray to keep me from freezing;
> Yonder I shall live in light and warmth for ever…
> Here I can have the world,
> There I shall have thee in Christ…
> Here are gross comforts, more burden than benefit,
> There is joy without sorrow…
> Rest without weariness.
> Give me to know that heaven is all love…
> Heaven is all peace…
> Heaven is all joy.
> The end of believing, fasting, praying, mourning, hum-
>   bling, watching, fearing, repining;
> And lead me to it soon.*

I speak the words, and the room is breathless with Jesus. I feel Him. We feel Him. He is very much there and speaking, calling us all to His side. We are swept away in the moment of life and death and purpose and passion and *Why, God* and *Oh, God, help* and *Please, God, make my life matter.* We are a collective heap of tears and mucus-filled noses.

---

* Arthur Bennett, ed., *The Valley of Vision: A Collection of Puritan Prayers and Devotions* (Carlisle, PA: The Banner of Truth Trust, 1975), 370-71.

And I know, in that moment, Jenn is smiling. Because she is in that place of wanting no more.

My friends, we are still here. We are still on the journey. We are still needy and grasping and desperate for more of God than we even know. We are still trudging through bad days and soaring through good ones. We still have hope to be better than we were yesterday and the promise of grace if we are not. We still have the ability to influence. We still have the capacity to dream. We can still get this thing right, still say *I'm sorry*, still forgive, still pursue, still believe, still remember.

And until the day we go to swim in that big ocean, we can still love God more than we ever have and give Him more than we've ever given…and have the most amazing life of more than we've ever known.

Blog Post:
I Want God

My blog post from January 3, 2012—the day I came out of hiding in the safety of the daily tall-tree forest and decide to focus on God to get better.

For the next 30 days, my voice on this blog will be silent. It is something I did not go into 2012 intending to do.

I do not believe in resolutions any more than I believe God needs a man-made calendar to make anything new.

What I do believe in are commitments, surrender, and recognizing when God is messing with you and being willing to go publicly dark while He does what He privately needs to do.

I want God. That is where I am.

Even as I type this, I feel much less like the overtired housewife, dreading the treadmill...lamenting my to-do lists and the laundry piles that never seem to end.

Instead I feel like an old-time preacher, standing in the white canvas walls of a puffy tent, palms sweating in anticipation of the delivery of words. And like old-time preachers, my words may go long and I will seem unaware because I am consumed with the message.

Before I lay this blog down for a month, allow me to share what I believe He is telling me...for in it, maybe there is a word or two for you.

- Pursue Me in a full-on sprint, the kind where arms pump and legs race and at the end it is the good kind of exhausting.

- When you feel Me messing with you, let Me.

- Pay attention to the rumbling, even when things don't make sense, remembering that I don't usually work in any traditional way and that rumbling often represents an uprising of a spiritual kind.

- Don't fear what others may think or say, as that is a terroristic tactic of Satan meant to take you out of the game altogether.

- Have integrity, even when it costs you something else.

- Stop wasting time trying to fix yourself when that introspection costs you prolonged time out in the field, pointing people to Me. You know enough. Now just go.

- Dive in, sometimes blindly. Do the hard thing without knowledge of how it will play out. Say no to things your freedom allows but at the end of the day won't make you more holy.

- Lay things down and simply walk away. Offer praise in moments of pain. Live the Word, once and for all.

- Stop giving excuses for why your way works better. Know the difference between human imperfection and when "I'm messy" becomes a crutch.

- Endure, not in the quick-fix way the world promotes but in the kind of raw, rogue Old Testament way that made regular people heroes.

- Know that nothing works but Me and quit wasting time pretending it does.

- Realize that what you grasp the tightest is what you most

need to release and that I honor doing hard things first rather than last resorts.

- Chase only the accomplishment of loving Me more than anything else.

My friends, I dive into 2012 not knowing what else Jesus may say. I enter my 30 days with Him expectantly, believing that in my stillness He will continue to be loud. And as always, I will share those things with you as He prompts.

In the meantime, will you join me in saying…**I want God.**

Lisa Whittle is a natural leader and bold thinker. Her refreshing, bottom-line approach appeals to audiences across the nation as she points them to a passionate pursuit of God. Lisa's past experiences include writing stints with Catalyst and Women of Faith, church planting, national media appearances, and traveling with Compassion International. Lisa is a wife and mother of three who currently resides in North Carolina. Visit her at www.lisawhittle.com.

To learn more about Lisa Whittle
or to read sample chapters,
visit www.harvesthousepublishers.com